T0326406

Entrepreneurship
in the **Arab World**

Entrepreneurship
in the Arab World
Ten Case Studies

**El-Khazindar Business Research
and Case Center**

The American University in Cairo Press
Cairo New York

First published in 2016 by
The American University in Cairo Press
113 Sharia Kasr el Aini, Cairo, Egypt
420 Fifth Avenue, New York, NY 10018
www.aucpress.com

Exclusive distribution outside Egypt and North America by I.B.Tauris & Co Ltd., 6 Salem Road, London, W4 2BU

Dar el Kutub No. 14009/14
ISBN 978 977 416 700 3

Dar el Kutub Cataloging-in-Publication Data

El-Khazindar Business Research and Case Center
    Entrepreneurship in the Arab World: Ten Case Studies / El-Khazindar Business Research and Case Center.—Cairo: The American University in Cairo Press, 2016.
    p. cm.
    ISBN 978 977 416 700 3
    1. Entrepreneurship—Middle East
    2. Entrepreneurship—North Africa
    338.04

1 2 3 4 5   20 19 18 17 16

Designed by Jon W. Stoy
Printed in Egypt

Contents

Contributors

Ali Awni is an associate professor of practice in the School of Business at the American University in Cairo, where he teaches operations management courses at both undergraduate and MBA levels. He was previously the head of the Qualifying Industrial Zones (QIZ) Unit at the Egyptian Ministry of Trade and Industry, as well as the supply chain consulting services at KPMG Hazem Hassan in Egypt. Dr. Awni obtained extensive management consulting, system development, and operations research experience in the United States, and now holds a BSc in computer science and statistics from Kuwait University, an MS in systems science from the University of Ottawa, and a PhD in operations research from North Carolina State University.

Aliaa Bassiouny is an assistant professor of finance at the American University in Cairo, teaching undergraduate and graduate courses in finance, investment analysis, and portfolio management. She is also the director of the Master of Science in Finance program, and the associate chair of the Department of Management. Bassiouny holds a BBA and an MBA, both with a specialization in finance, from the American University in Cairo. She also earned her Master in Research (MRes) and PhD from ESADE Business School in Barcelona, Spain.

Manar El-Batrawy is a treasury assistant at GlaxoSmithKline. She is currently working towards a Master of Science in Finance at the American University in Cairo, studying corporate finance, financial modeling, financial econometrics, and financial institutions and markets. She earned her bachelor's degree in business administration, with concentration in finance, from the American University in Cairo.

Laura Guindy graduated from the American University in Cairo with a degree in economics and a minor in business administration. She is currently working at an IT company called EMC, and is hoping to pursue her master's degree in economics.

Abderrahman Hassi teaches management at Al Akhawayn University in Morocco. He was previously a professor at Algonquin College in Ottawa, Canada, and taught numerous employee training courses, particularly programs for employees of the federal public service of Canada. His primary research interests include business case study methods, employee training management, and cross-cultural management.

Rania S. Hussein is assistant professor of marketing in the School of Business at the American University in Cairo. She received her MBA from Georgia State University in 2001, and her PhD from the University of Nottingham in 2010. Her research interests include internet marketing, social media, and innovation adoption.

Ayman Ismail is assistant professor and Jameel Endowed Chair of Entrepreneurship at the School of Business at the American University in Cairo. He has led the school's Entrepreneurship and Innovation Program (EIP), and founded the AUC Venture Lab. Prior to that, he was a research fellow at Harvard University, and a consultant with McKinsey & Company and the World Bank/IFC. He holds a PhD in international economic development and a master's degree from MIT, and a BSc in engineering and an MBA from AUC. In 2012, he was selected as a Young Global Leader by the World Economic Forum.

Brendon Johnson is a research assistant at the American University in Cairo, where he researches and writes on issues related to both business and social entrepreneurship in Egypt. He also regularly consults with Egyptian start-ups on strategic and organizational management, revenue generation, and marketing. Since 2011, Brendon has worked directly with early-stage social entrepreneurs in Egypt through the incubator Nahdet El Mahrousa, serving also as the director of university programs at the social start-up The Nile Project. Johnson is also the co-founder of the social enterprise Baladini. He holds an MA in development studies from the University of Hong Kong and a BA in political science from West Chester University.

Nagwan Ibrahim Farage Lashin has extensive experience in the oil and gas industry. She established Amar ya Masr, a social enterprise aiming to transform poor women's lives by teaching them skills enabling them to earn their own money. Lashin holds a BA in english literature from Helwan University, a project management diploma from the Institute of Project Management of Ireland, and an MBA from Maastricht School of Management.

Ashraf A. Mahate is the head of export market intelligence at Dubai Exports, which is an agency of the Dubai Department of Economic Development. Previously, he taught economics, finance, entrepreneurship, and innovation at universities in the United Kingdom and in the UAE.

Hend Mostafa graduated from the American University in Cairo with a major in business administration, with a concentration in marketing and a minor in psychology, and completed her MBA, also from the American University in Cairo, with a marketing concentration. She has both presented and published a number of business case studies over the course of her career.

Maha Mourad is associate professor of marketing, and the former director of El-Khazindar Business Research and Case Center (KCC) in the Department of Management in the School of Business at the American University in Cairo (AUC). She holds a BA and an MBA from AUC, and a PhD in marketing from the University of Nottingham. Her research interests include brand equity, service marketing, innovation marketing, and higher education marketing. Her professional experience includes several national and regional consultancy assignments.

Sanjai K. Parahoo is the director for postgraduate programs at the Business School of Hamdan Bin Mohammed Smart University in Dubai. He has extensive research experience in various African countries. He teaches courses in marketing and innovation strategies. His publications focus on the investigation of antecedents and consequences of consumer engagement in business and e-learning environments.

Iman Seoudi is an assistant professor of strategic management and entrepreneurship and the director of El-Khazindar Business Research and Case Center (KCC) at the American University in Cairo. She holds BA and MA degrees from AUC, and a PhD in strategic management from Case Western Reserve University. Her research interests include public policy, promoting venture capital and innovative business models in Egypt and the Arab world, as well as corporate social responsibility and ethical perceptions and behavior of business students and executives. She has been involved in several entrepreneurship development programs over the course of her career.

Mirette A. Shoeir holds a business administration degree from the American University in Cairo. She has worked on the public relations team of RIM, and is currently completing her MA in theatre studies at York University in Toronto.

Ali Soliman received a BSc (Honors) from Cairo University, an MA from the American University in Cairo, and a PhD in economics from the University of Iowa. He has had wide exposure to international affairs and development issues during his tenure with the World Bank in Washington, DC, as adviser to the governments of the Maldives and the Kingdom of Saudi Arabia, and as CEO/general manager of ICD, a regional financial organization concerned with the development of the private sector in Africa, Asia, and Southern Europe. He has also held senior posts in the Ministries of Economy and International Cooperation in Egypt. He currently teaches economics at the British University in Egypt.

Acknowledgments

In acknowledgment of the dedicated individuals who made this casebook possible, El-Khazindar Business Research and Case Center (KCC) would first like to thank Dr. Nigel Fletcher-Jones, director of the American University in Cairo Press, for his dedication, openness, and professionalism in producing such an excellent casebook. With Dr. Fletcher-Jones's wise leadership, the AUC Press is publishing a business casebook for the very first time, collaborating with KCC in producing an inspirational and useful business source for the entire Middle East and North Africa region. We would also like to extend our deep thanks to Neil Hewison, the associate director for the AUC Press's editorial programs, for his unwavering dedication, support, and flexibility throughout this entire process.

It is an honor for us to send our genuine thanks to Dr. Salah Hassan, professor of global brand management at the George Washington School of Business, for his invaluable expert and supportive role as this casebook's editor in chief. His continuous encouragement and positive reinforcement provided this project with a tremendous sense of purpose, igniting both creativity and hard work.

In addition, we would like to thank all the reviewers, English editors, and the KCC team, who contributed terrifically towards the successful completion of the manuscript. The publication of this casebook would not have been possible without the insight and scrutiny of the brilliant editorial team.

Finally, we would like to thank Dr. Karim Seghir, dean of the School of Business at the American University in Cairo (AUC), for his ongoing support and encouragement. From the very start of this project, Dr. Seghir has been passionately overseeing all the processes necessary to ensure the best possible outcome.

Maha Mourad, Former Director
El-Khazindar Business Research and Case Center
School of Business, American University in Cairo

Foreword

The use of business cases has significantly increased since the 1980s, becoming an integral part of business education, particularly in developed countries. Business cases have been proven to be beneficial for both academia and the corporate sector. More precisely, case studies represent an effective teaching tool that brings up-to-date real life practices to the academic sphere, while ensuring a very dynamic, engaging, and participant-centered learning environment. Case-based pedagogy also provides tangible examples of why businesses succeed or fail in a variety of sectors and contexts. Furthermore, business schools have been committed, especially in the past couple of decades, to narrowing the gap between the corporate sector and academia. Business cases represent an excellent bridge between academia and the business community, endowing students with practical knowledge and preparing them to become successful members in an increasingly competitive market. Often a significant knowledge gap emerges between the skills obtained in academia and their applicability to practical, real-life scenarios. The use of case studies is incredibly beneficial because it directly combats this problem, minimizing the gap. Moreover, their use is crucial for successful companies to strengthen their reputation, provide a testimonial of their success, and become a leader in the field by allowing others to emulate their strategies. Improving relations between academia and the corporate world since the 1980s have brought a new era, completely redefining the interactions between the two fields and in turn benefitting society as a whole.

Although the use of business cases in the Arab region increased in the past decade, most of the cases have been produced in western countries, and therefore do not accurately reflect the specific business environment in the region. The Arab region is undergoing significant political and economic transformations, and the business environment has been adapting and rising to the challenges and opportunities generated. The recent events in the region provide an unprecedented window of opportunity for economic reforms, private enterprise development, and sustainable business. Amid these unique dynamics, the need for producing and disseminating local business cases has become more critical than ever, as they provide business leaders and policy makers with pertinent knowledge about the complex, resourceful, and ever-changing business environment in the region. Furthermore, the field of academia in the region must adapt to the recent transformations by using business cases to apply academic skills to the ever-changing political and economic environment of the Arab region. The School of Business of the American University in Cairo is committed to playing a leading role in producing and disseminating glocalized knowledge. By combining the essence and advantages of a globalized approach rooted in the local context in order to reflect the needs, challenges, opportunities, and cultural characteristics specific to the Arab region, the School seeks to become a regional leader in the advancement of locally produced business cases in order to catalyze growth in the societies of the Arab region as a whole.

The Arab region is characterized by a very young population, over half of which is below the age of 25. Youth unemployment in the region is approximately 24%, nearly double the world's average rate and the highest regional youth unemployment rate in the world. Around 29% of total employment is filled by the public sector. The private sector in the Arab region, therefore, needs to be strengthened to absorb more of the youth workforce. A well-directed entrepreneurship ecosystem appertaining to innovation and creativity is crucial in providing a sustainable solution for the region's most pressing challenge: youth unemployment. Although research shows that scalable start-ups are key for job creation, most start-ups in the region are unscalable due to the lack of young entrepreneurs combining innovation and creativity with professional skills necessary to scale-up small businesses, and the absence of applicable literature, focused specifically on the region, to draw from. This emphasizes the importance of taking business education outside the classroom back into the market for entrepreneurship, which this book does well.

This book focuses on social entrepreneurship and innovation in the Arab region and provides an assortment of research-based business cases that address key issues such as start-ups, growth, expansion, sell-outs, re-launch, and exits. It covers different industries related to food service, telecommunications, banking, and manufacturing in various Arab countries, including Egypt, Morocco, the United Arab Emirates, and Saudi Arabia. I am confident that this book will have an impactful contribution and ultimately benefit the Arab region as a whole.

I would like to take this opportunity to thank the authors, the reviewers, and the editors of this book for their invaluable contribution and for sharing their expertise. This book is intended to serve as a knowledge resource for business leaders, policymakers, scholars, entrepreneurs, and family business owners in the Arab region and developing economies across the world. The ultimate goal of the book is to nurture a sustainable entrepreneurial environment rooted in innovation and creativity and to contribute to minimizing youth unemployment in the region.

Karim Seghir, Dean
School of Business, American University in Cairo

Introduction

It is a great privilege to be serving as Editor-in-Chief for the first Entrepreneurship Casebook, written in collaboration with the American University in Cairo Press (AUC Press) and the El Khazindar Business Research and Case Center (KCC), at the School of Business of the American University in Cairo (AUC). The Arab World is one with a dire need for proactive entrepreneurship–business innovation that seeks to meet society's most unspoken needs, providing new job opportunities, and improving the economy. As the world advances, technologies dominate, and economies diversify, countries race against time to become more competitive while providing a better quality of life for their citizens. Newer and more pressing problems emerge that require innovative and entrepreneurial solutions. As a result, business schools around the world are facing the challenging reality of integrating innovation with entrepreneurial solutions. The School of Business at the American University in Cairo is not an exception in recognizing that rising entrepreneurs must be focused on innovation in order to develop creative business startups that meet the needs of the market within their own region, so as to be able to contribute responsibly with practical, sustainable, and creative solutions.

It is therefore with great pride that I present to you this casebook, compiled specifically for the purpose of entrepreneurial exposure and integration into the startup market. Over the last three years, the Arab World has experienced major changes and challenging new realities, collectively calling for civil engagement and raising awareness for social responsibility. The Arab Spring is therefore in the current process of appeasing the discontent and meeting public demand. There is no doubt that the youth holds the power for effective change. As a result, KCC has recognized that an appropriate place to start would be at the very beginning. For decades on end, educational facilities have been consumed with implanting theoretical concepts into the minds of their students; and while in and of themselves these hypotheses and ideals are valid, true practical influence cannot rest on them alone. It is for this reason that the School of Business at the American University in Cairo, and the KCC, have finally decided to bridge the gap between theory and practice, expediting the proactive change-making process.

Essentially, entrepreneurship has always been a part of society: no need has ever gone unmet as long as we've retained the ability to fulfill it. This volume consists of a total of ten case studies, exploring startups of all business fields, that each tell the story of an individual, or a group, who proactively rose to meet specific societal needs. At a time when many businesses suffered the complete demise of their projects as a result of social pressures, many cases presented throughout this casebook exhibit the strong-willed dedication of the bright entrepreneurs who managed to engage their problem-solving skills in the salvaging of their dreams. Authors Ayman Ismail and Brendon Johnson write a case study about the famous Egyptian optic chain Baraka Optics, exploring the struggles that it faced as a result of the Egyptian revolution. When the economy dropped, so did the sales; and when the sales dropped, the company's instability rose. Still, Ahmed Ragab, the chain's CEO, managed to incorporate new strategies into his business, and picked the company back up on its feet. Other entrepreneurs, such as Ahmed Dakrouri, were able to utilize the miserly economic situation in Egypt for the innovation of their proactive startups. Authors Nagwan Ibrahim and Ali H. Awni explore the case of Horticulture and Social Enterprise in Minya, Egypt, telling of how Dakrouri was able to provide farmers with a source of income, while symbiotically benefiting his local Egyptian economy. Moreover, inducing a new business (no matter how small) into the market is often likened to bringing a child into the world. Before the project enters into the real world and is able to flourish on its own, the entrepreneurs behind it go through "birthing pains"—certain struggles and obstacles that arise at the very start. Ashraf A. Mahate and Sanjai K. Parahoo provide a case study on Abdulla Mohammed's struggle with integrating a creative coffee shop into the already existing hospitality sector of the UAE market. Undergoing his own "birthing pains" Mohammed must figure out a way by which to introduce novelty along with his idea. Meanwhile, startups such as Ariika Bean Bags, Bey2ollak traffic app, and Choco'a, face different obstacles as they embrace their thriving success, and consider ways by which to expand and develop.

All great businesses merely start with an idea; it is the evolution of that idea that needs inspiration and motivation to see it through. The hope is that this casebook will be able to provide entrepreneurs, business leaders, students, and educators, with a firm understanding of the Arab business marketplace as it currently stands, exposing entrepreneurs to a solid source of inspiration from which they might commit to their creative ideas and take their small businesses to the next level. Startups such as Funlozia and Abdelkader Mouaziz's Tourtite B&B serve as inspiration to the fact that with the right exposure and market research, entrepreneurs can see to it that the smallest of their ideas are implemented. Even with franchising an already-existent brand (such as Olives and ICD, also featured in this casebook), an entrepreneurial talent serves an influential function in the emerging economies of the Arab World. Entrepreneurs face the challenge and responsibility of shaping decisions that will influence their society. This is the first volume of an engaging series whose main and ultimate objective is to better the Arab World and advance its competitiveness while improving the quality of life of its own citizens.

Salah S. Hassan,
Professor of Global Brand Management
George Washington University

1 Ariika Beanbags: A Successful Egyptian Entrepreneur Capable of Regional Expansion?

Rania S. Hussein and Hend Mostafa

Macroeconomic Overview of Egypt[1]

The richness of the Nile River that crosses Egypt, together with its central location at the northeast corner of Africa, has made Egypt an influential country in the Middle East. During the presidency of Gamal Abd al-Nasser, Egypt's economy was highly centralized. This changed to an open-door policy in the 1970s under former president Anwar al-Sadat. Between 2004 and 2008, former president Hosni Mubarak pursued economic reforms to attract foreign investment and increase GDP. Economic growth in recent years was not reflected in living conditions, however. After the revolution in January 2011, the government increased social spending to address people's dissatisfaction, but political uncertainty reduced economic growth and affected many sectors, such as tourism, manufacturing, and construction. Unemployment increased and economic growth is likely to remain slow due to the unstable political environment in Egypt.

In 2013, Egypt's GDP per capita was US$6,600, a 1.8 percent increase from the previous year. The unemployment rate reached 13.4 percent and the inflation rate increased from 7.1 percent in 2012 to 9 percent in 2013. Egypt's exports in 2013 reached $24.81 billion while imports were $59.22 billion. The main exports are crude oil and petroleum products, cotton, textiles, metal products, chemicals, and processed food. Machinery and equipment, foodstuffs, chemicals, wood products, and fuels are imported products.

The Furniture Industry in Egypt[2]

The furniture industry in Egypt has a long history based on the strength of Egyptians' craftsmanship. During the French and British colonial periods, Egyptian craftsmen were influenced by the European styles, which were reflected in their furniture production. The Europeans encouraged the industry's development in the port city of Damietta, where it flourished. The Egyptian furniture industry witnessed its largest boom when it started exporting to the Middle East and North Africa (MENA) between 2004 and 2005 (fig. 1.1). In 2004, Egypt's furniture exports were $48 million; in 2010 they reached $255 million. The MENA region was considered to be the best export destination for Egyptian furniture as they share a similar history, culture, and consumer preferences. In 2009, Saudi Arabia imported $61 million of Egyptian furniture products, which represents 23 percent of Egyptian furniture exports. The United Arab Emirates is the second largest export destination, with $22.2 million of Egyptian furniture exports (fig. 1.2). Between 2005 and 2009, exports to Europe increased. While Egypt exported finished products to MENA countries, exports to European countries consisted of unfinished products sourced by European manufacturers. As the demand for furniture in the local market increased, Egypt's imports of furniture also increased. In 2009, Egypt's imports from China, for example, reached $55 million.

Fig. 1.1. The boom in the furniture industry in Egypt

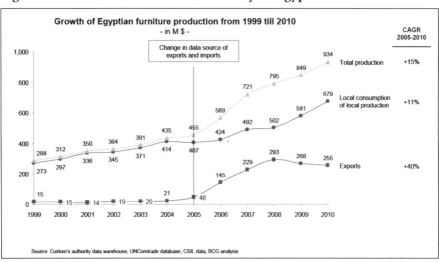

Source: Industrial Modernization Center, "Egyptian Furniture Sector Development Strategy," December 2010, http://www.egytrade.be/wp-content/uploads/2013/03/Egypt-Furniture-Report-02-2011-1.pdf

Fig. 1.2. Top export destinations for furniture from Egypt, 2009

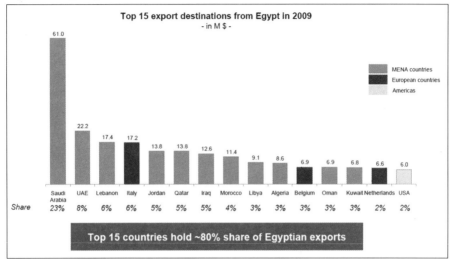

Source: Industrial Modernization Center, "Egyptian Furniture Sector Development Strategy," December 2010, http://www.egytrade.be/wp-content/uploads/2013/03/Egypt-Furniture-Report-02-2011-1.pdf

In 2009, the production of furniture reached $3 billion and exports were $296 million. The furniture market in Egypt is divided between large companies that focus on exports and small companies that focus on the local market. The small local producers represent most of the market.[3] Several factors were behind the boom in the furniture industry in Egypt. Firstly, there is the strong and recognized know-how of woodworking in Egypt. Secondly, the geographical location of Egypt and the cultural proximity to Europe and the MENA countries gave Egypt a special advantage. Moreover, the Egyptian furniture manufacturers were willing to produce small quantities to fill specific market gaps or customize products according to customers' preferences, which increased demand for Egyptian furniture. Finally, Egyptian furniture products have very attractive prices compared to those of other countries. This is mainly due to the low labor cost in Egypt, which was $2 per hour in 2009, compared to $14.90 in the United States and $18.80 in France. Another reason for the low cost of Egyptian furniture is the advantage that Egypt possesses in shipping cost and transit time, because of its geographical proximity to the MENA countries and to Europe.

Despite these advantages, the Egyptian furniture market faces many challenges. One of the greatest is the fragmentation of the industry. The presence of only a few large players hinders the ability to develop further due to limited finance options. The limited quantities of furniture produced and the few varieties available are also obstacles to further growth. A factor that hinders international furniture manufacturers from investing in Egypt is the lack of copyright protections. The low productivity of labor in Egypt counteracts the country's low labor cost advantage. Despite these challenges, the furniture industry in Egypt is growing and opportunities still exist in many untapped markets.

Company Background

In 2010, four students at the American University of Cairo (Hassan Arslan, Shaher Arslan, Khaled Attallah, and Mohamed Bahgat) decided to develop their own business. They conducted research in order to determine what they should produce. Attallah, traveled to the United Kingdom as an exchange student, where he found beanbags used as furniture throughout university campuses and labs. The comfortable and practical beanbags encouraged Attallah to consider producing a similar product in Egypt. Since there were no branded beanbags in Egypt, the four students decided that introducing a high-quality branded beanbag could be a great opportunity. The four students decided to create the company Ariika, with the goal of developing a high-quality product at reasonable prices.

The Product

The brand name Ariika, which means 'sofa' in classical Arabic, was chosen to reflect the products that the company manufactures. The products are made of leather or are waterproof, with PVC coating. The beanbags are filled with Styrofoam developed specially for Ariika. This high-quality Styrofoam is more durable than the ordinary Styrofoam available in the market, and Ariika also sells Styrofoam separately for refilling and maintenance.

Although Ariika started by producing only beanbags, it now has four different products: beanbags, floating bags, floating mats, and a U-pillow. Ariika's products also allow for customization. At an additional charge, orders can be customized in terms of shape, color, images, or writing. The company has nine different designs of beanbags: five floating bags, three floating mats, and one U-pillow design. Ariika provides a one-year warranty for repair or replacement on its products.

Core Competency

Ariika produces the best value of branded beanbags in Egypt. They are of high quality, are reasonably priced, and have acceptable delivery time.

Ariika's products are not considered its core competency, however. Rather, it is the customer service and folllow-up that the company provides. Ariika's website is user-friendly, with all details about the products, colors, and offers available. The moment that a customer places an order, he or she receives a personalized email confirming the order. At each stage of the production process, an email is sent to the customer indicating where the order is. Ariika provides the option of tracking the order at any time, too. It also provides electronic invoices and warranties. Ariika thus differentiates itself from competitors by providing a special experience to its customers. Many customers believe that Ariika is a multinational company. "We operate on multinational standards; that's why we are perceived as one," remarked Arslan.

Target Markets

Ariika has three target markets: consumer, corporate, and resellers. Its consumer profile consists of youth 20 to 35 years old from the upper and upper-middle social classes. The company targets newlyweds who are looking for different furniture options for their homes. Ariika also targets university students; it has marketed its products at the American University in Cairo (AUC), the German University in Cairo (GUC), and the British University in Egypt (BUE). According to the CEO, the company achieved a market share of 50 percent of the branded beanbag market in Egypt in 2013.

In 2011, the year Ariika was launched, Coca-Cola approached them and ordered 200 beanbags with its company logo to use in its marketing campaign. This opened a new target market for Ariika, and the company started targeting the corporate sector to strengthen its position in the market and build on its success. As Attallah indicated, "the barriers to entry are low; any company with enough financial resources could present a threat to Ariika." Pursuing the corporate market would allow Ariika to sustain its position in the market. By the end of 2011, Ariika was selling its products to Coca-Cola and to real estate companies like Mountain View and Palm Hills. In 2013, Ariika introduced its new floating bag, which was requested by both Coca-Cola and Pepsi for their marketing campaigns. There was a bidding war between the two companies and Pepsi won the bid. Accordingly, Ariika produced a thousand floating bags for Pepsi. The company's sales grew and, in 2013, it achieved a market share of 80 percent of the corporate market. Currently Ariika has many satisfied corporate clients, such as Vodafone, Etisalat, Coca-Cola, Pepsi, Heineken, Google, Bianchi Beach, Hilton, the Mountain View compound, Palm Hills, In & Out Furniture, and Danone.

Since its launch in 2011, Ariika has sold its products online through the company's website. In 2012, Ariika decided to expand and target customers who buy from furniture outlets. After successful negotiations, Ariika was able to display its products in furniture outlets such as In & Out Furniture, For Kare, Istikbal, and others. Ariika has sold large quantities of beanbags to beaches, cafés, and compounds. It also displays its products at online resellers such as Souq and Jumia. Currently the company controls 90 percent of the reseller market.

Marketing Strategy

The company's founders invested considerable time and effort in developing the brand name and image. They started by associating Ariika's brand name with comfort, quality, and customization. Later, they decided to focus on comfort to differentiate the company from future competitors. Ariika always highlighted the innovative designs and high quality of its products in its marketing campaigns to build a strong brand image. In May 2011, Ariika was introduced at the AUC campus under the campaign "Try Me and Buy Me." Ariika products were distributed around the AUC campus and students were allowed to try the beanbag and place orders. Although the company's forecast sales for the first month were thirty beanbags, actual sales were 130.

The company's sales continued to grow and it invested in any marketing opportunity available. Ariika implemented its marketing plans at private universities in Egypt such as AUC, GUC, and BUE, targeting the young people who study there. Through these campaigns, the company introduced its brand and allowed customers to try its products.

Ariika relied heavily on online marketing. The company developed a website where customers could customize, place, and track their orders. It also used social media tools such as Facebook, Twitter, and Instagram to promote its products. Through social media, customers can interact with Ariika, ask questions, and provide feedback. At the same time Ariika can announce new offers, introduce new products, or promote new events directly to its customers. Thanks to its extensive online presence, Ariika had 91,090 likes on Facebook in 2014, the highest of any beanbag company in the world. Fat Boy, the most popular beanbag brand globally, had only 32,607 likes.

According to Hassan Arslan, before 2013, the company had no clearly defined marketing budget and the marketing expenditures were not closely tracked, which resulted in some decisions that had a negative impact on the company's profits. Arslan decided to focus more on budgeting and allocated a specific budget to the different functions at Ariika. With time and thorough training, the owners were able to develop more systematic ways of allocating their expenditures and determining what resources would be allocated to which function. This, according to Arslan, reduced redundancy and increased efficiency. Currently Ariika places its advertisements on social media, as they are the best method to reach its target market. Moreover, the effect of online ads can be monitored and evaluated easily, unlike for other, more expensive offline marketing.

Ariika marketed its products in *Enigma* magazine, which has an online store that sells furniture and clothing, and on Nefsak.com, an e-commerce website. Ariika also appeared in two major furniture exhibitions in Egypt: Le Marché 2011 and La Casa. These exhibitions allowed the company to introduce its products to many visitors.

Production Strategy

Production was one of the most challenging functions for Ariika. The main problems were limited capacity and huge waste. When the company started in 2011, its capacity was three beanbags per day. As demand increased, the company faced many delays in the production process and delivery. The high demand from the corporate market was an added burden. "Supply was always lower than demand," recalled Arslan. The company started considering different options to satisfy the increasing demand, outsourcing some of its operations to small sewing workshops; however, this negatively affected the quality of the beanbag. To overcome this issue, Ariika began providing specific standards to its suppliers in order to assure the quality of the beanbag.

The company worked on increasing the in-house production capacity by reducing waste and increasing efficiency. In 2012, Ariika was able to produce 200 beanbags a day. Although revenues increased in 2012, profits were lower than in 2011. Arslan decided to focus more on reducing costs. By evaluating the production process, Arslan found that for every three beanbags produced, one was wasted, which added to costs and reduced production capacity. He focused on increasing the efficiency of the production process to reduce waste, which minimized costs.

Supply Chain Management

Supply chain management is also a challenge for Ariika. Currently the company is dealing with just a few suppliers, who are only accessible through their stores located in al-Azhar in Old Cairo. They are not available online and cannot be contacted through email, which increases the burden on the company, especially as Ariika is following the Just In Time system, whereby production starts when the order is placed. Moreover, the suppliers' leather, which they buy from China in large batches, is of inconsistent quality. Arslan is willing to pay more for higher-quality leather but it is not available in the market. This problem is controlled to some extent through strict inspection of the quality of leather that will go into the production of the beanbags.

Another problem that Arslan faces with suppliers is inconsistency in the size of Styrofoam. Suppliers provide either 3mm or 6mm Styrofoam according to availability. The size of the filling affects the number of kilograms (either 3 or 4) required for each beanbag. Therefore it is difficult for Arslan to predict the cost of the beanbag; it could be either LE100 or LE120 depending on the size of the Styrofoam available. Arslan is continuously searching for reliable suppliers who can provide him with a consistent size of Styrofoam.

Human Resources
The company was founded by four students at AUC. Due to the limited time at their disposition, they worked part-time in Ariika. Later, when they started hiring employees at the company, they depended more on students who work as part-timers and require low salaries. This option was convenient for Ariika's management due to initial budget constraints. However, although part-time employees cost less, they work less and are more difficult to monitor. As Ariika grew in the Egyptian market and revenues increased, the management considered employing full-time workers. Currently the production department employs full-time workers; other departments still depend on part-timers.

Distribution
When Ariika was launched in 2011, it sold its products through its website. In 2012, the company aimed at penetrating the retail market and sold its products at different furniture outlets. Building on its success, Arslan decided to create the first Ariika store in 2013. The store was located on the North Coast, where Ariika's target market spends the summer. Although the store operated for only three weeks, the company was able to break even and make some profit. Arslan is currently considering opening two new Ariika stores.

Ariika has a very professional delivery system. The company owns two trucks and delivers its products to customers' homes ten days after the order is placed. "When Ariika started targeting corporate there was a delay in delivery to our customers," Arslan mentioned. That was mainly due to the large volumes required by corporate clients. Arslan was able to over-come these problems by outsourcing production at peak times. By doing that, Ariika was able to fix its delivery date to within ten days from the placement of the orders. Each day of the week is dedicated to delivering orders to specific areas in Cairo.

Finance

Ariika started its business with a total of LE8,000, invested as follows: LE3,000 to develop the website, LE2,000 to buy the machine, and LE3,000 for materials. Within three days of its marketing campaign 'Try Me and Buy Me,' the company sold a lot of beanbags, broke even, and started making a profit. The company started to face challenges related to finance, however. Having minimal experience in this area, the founders faced many difficulties with respect to budgeting and preparing income statements and cash flow statements. In the first year, the founders decided to distribute all profits as dividends to the founders. This decision was later considered unwise by Arslan: "We should have kept some profits to reinvest in the company." Arslan spent more than a year reading books about accounting and finance. As a result he was able to prepare income statements and cash flow statements that allowed him to have a clear view of Ariika's current position. As shown in table 1.1, Ariika's revenues increased between 2011 and 2013; however, profits were lower in 2012 than in 2011. This decrease was alarming to Arslan, who started monitoring what was behind the high increase in cost. Production inefficiency at the beginning was the main reason for the decrease in profits. After it improved the efficiency of the production process, Ariika's profits increased again. In 2014, Arslan started identifying specific budgets for each function in the company. He believed that budgeting and forecasting would allow him to make more sounder, monitor the company's performance better, and increase profits.

Table 1.1. Ariika's revenues and profits, 2011–13

	2011	2012	2013
Revenues (LE)	650,000	1,200,000	2,000,000
Costs (LE)	475,000	1,080,000	1,300,000
Profit (LE)	175,000	120,000	700,000

Source: Company records

External Challenges: Competition

Changes in the external environment had major effects on Ariika. One of these changes was competition in the local and international markets. There are four main competitors for Ariika in the local market—Antakh, Cozy Bean Bags, B Bags, and Maniera—and one international competitor, Fat Boy.

Antakh was the first competitor to enter the market after Ariika. It had produced beanbags for some time before Ariika appeared. Those beanbags were unbranded, however, and were sold in Kasr Bayan, an outlet that sells curtains and fabrics. In 2012, the success of Ariika encouraged owners of the company to replicate its model, and they started branding the beanbags produced by Kasr Bayan as Antakh. Antakh was sold at different outlets and had a very fast delivery date of four days after the placement of the orders. The company sold a wide range of beanbags with different colors and materials such as leather, cotton, and waterproof. Antakh also provided customization options to its clients and currently it has one store in Cairo.

B Bags was developed by a group of BUE students who wanted to win a share of Ariika's success. B Bags has a very slow delivery date, though, of 13 days after the placement of the order. The company produces different products such as beanbags, pillows, lounges, chairs, and buffs.

Cozy was founded in 2012. The company aims at producing quality beanbags in a variety of shapes and colors. Cozy sold its products at La Vista (North Coast), Spinneys hypermarket, and Wadi Degla Health Club.[4] Maniera is yet another competitor; customers place their orders by telephone. Cozy and Maniera are considered very weak competitors, so Ariika focuses more on Antakh and B Bags, as they have quality products and are actively trying to increase their market share.

Fat Boy began in the Netherlands in 2002. The company started by producing a lounge chair designed for fashion and comfort. After its success, the company introduced a wider range of beanbags that were developed in a European style with creative designs. The company's philosophy is to 'delete dull' by providing a unique experience to its customers. The company aims to change customers' perceptions and improve their lifestyle by introducing innovative and unique products. Fat Boy has no stores in Egypt but it sells its products through resellers. Currently the company sells its products to more than sixty countries worldwide.[5]

Initial Exporting Attempts

In 2013, Arslan decided to export Ariika's products internationally. He had many connections in the United States and he decided to begin there.

"We didn't conduct any research before going to the United States; we found an opportunity and we decided to grab it," Arslan said. The lack of knowledge about the U.S. market affected the company negatively. The first obstacle that the company faced was the large size of the beanbags. One hundred beanbags was enough to fill a 12 meter container, which increased transportation costs. After reaching the U.S. market, Ariika's beanbag was sold for US$200 to accommodate the high costs of transportation. "Our exports to the United States were a total failure," recalled Arslan. "We sold our beanbags for $200 while competitors sold theirs for only $80." He decided to stop exporting to the United States and started considering other alternatives.

After his failure in the U.S. market, Arslan searched for expert advice to help his company move forward. In 2013, Endeavor, an NGO that focuses on high-impact entrepreneurs, chose Ariika to be among the entrepreneurial firms that it would support. Although the final selection is not yet over, Arslan has met a number of mentors and business experts who encouraged him to consider the Middle East market as the first step for Ariika's international expansion. Following their advice, in 2014, Arslan decided to do extensive research on countries in the Middle East, looking specifically at Lebanon as an opportunity for Ariika to expand.

Arslan traveled to Lebanon to get a better idea of the market there. He met several distributors and was considering semi-FDI (foreign direct investment) as a mode of entry. He decided to export empty beanbags to minimize the huge space taken up by the full beanbag. The filling would be added in Lebanon and the beanbag could be sold there. "One filled beanbag was equivalent to 100 empty beanbags," explained Arslan. "Accordingly, exporting empty ones will reduce the shipping costs." Ariika beanbags will be sold in Lebanon for 80 Lebanese liras while competitors sell at 400 Lebanese liras. Although Lebanon is a very attractive market, Arslan decided to postpone his expansion plan for some time due to political instability and security issues in Lebanon.

Ariika Moving Forward

Although the expansion plan for Lebanon was postponed, Arslan was thinking of expanding to other markets in the Middle East. He would need to conduct extensive research before introducing Ariika to a new market. Another option is introducing an 'Ariika Home' line. Arslan wanted to invest in Ariika's strong name in Egypt and develop hard furniture under the name 'Ariika Home.' He was considering using the same approach as for

Table 1.2. Ariika's gross margin by product category (in LE)

Shape	Product category	Denim	PVC	Leather	Average variable cost	Price	Gross profit	Gross profit margin
Tod	beanbag	22	24	25	24	150	126	84%
Kids' floating mat	floating mat	18	20	0	19	200	181	91%
Mini mat	floating mat	49	57	0	53	250	197	79%
Kids' double mat	floating mat	27	31	0	29	300	271	90%
Kids	beanbag	78	83	0	81	395	314	80%
Floating mat	floating mat	54	62	0	58	400	342	86%
Medium standard	beanbag	92	102	0	97	450	353	78%
Mini couch	beanbag	70	78	76	75	450	375	83%
Sea lounger	beanbag	108	0	0	108	500	392	78%
C bag	floating beanbag	71	0	0	71	500	429	86%
Dolphy	floating beanbag	70	0	0	70	500	430	86%
Standard	beanbag	129	135	147	137	540	403	75%
Chair	beanbag	128	130	121	126	540	414	77%
Pumpkin	beanbag	133	145	162	147	585	438	75%
Double floating mat	floating mat	106	122	0	114	600	486	81%
Lexy	floating beanbag	110	0	0	110	600	490	82%
Hammer head	floating beanbag	100	0	0	100	600	500	83%
Lounger	beanbag	140	163	190	164	650	486	75%
Willow	beanbag	165	204	236	202	700	498	71%
Couch	beanbag	183	204	234	207	720	513	71%
Free Willy	floating beanbag	150	0	0	150	800	650	81%
Huge	beanbag	397	433	424	418	1,500	1,082	72%
Donut	floating mat	346	0	0	346	1,620	1,274	79%
U-pillow	U-pillow	0	0	14	14	100	86	86%

Source: Company records

'Ariika Comfort,' which was built on the concept of selling online. According to Arslan, there is a market gap for selling hard furniture online and he wants to seize this opportunity. In addition to expanding the company's portfolio, Arslan studied the possibility of increasing its reach in Egypt. He wanted to open more stores to sell Ariika's products at different places in Egypt. Each of these plans requires large investments and efforts and thus Arslan needs to focus. Should he take more steps in international expansion? If yes, which countries should he consider and which entry mode should he use? Saudi Arabia is a strong option, as four investors have approached Arslan so far. Should he expand his product portfolio and introduce hard furniture? If yes, should he introduce these products under Ariika Comfort or Ariika Home? Should Arslan stay focused on beanbags and alternative furniture or start branding furniture products? Should he focus more on the Egyptian market and open new stores or seek international expansion?

Notes

1 Central Intelligence Agency, *The World Fact Book*, https://www.cia.gov/library/publications/the-world-factbook/geos/eg.html
2 Industrial Modernization Center, "Egyptian Furniture Sector Development Strategy," December 2010, http://www.egytrade.be/wp-content/uploads/2013/03/Egypt-Furniture-Report-02-2011-1.pdf
3 Industrial Modernization Center, "Furniture and Wood Industries," 2009, http://www.imc-egypt.org/secfurniture.asp
4 Cozy Bean Bags, http://cozy-beanbags.com/about-u/
5 Fat Boy, http://fatboyusa.com/about/

2 Bey2ollak—Beat Traffic Together: A Case Study from Egypt

Maha Mourad and Laura Guindy

Bey2ollak is a crowd-sourced traffic application for smartphones. The idea seems simple and easy, so why was it such a big hit? Why did more than six thousand users download the application on the first day of its release alone? Bear in mind that the released version was for Blackberry smartphones only in addition to the normal Web version. Why do so many people continue to download it today? Why did *Daily News Egypt* describe it as "more essential to traffic than traffic lights?" What are the reasons for its success? Did the environment and setting in Egypt facilitate this success or make it more difficult? And most importantly: is it sustainable? This calls for a closer look and analysis of the environment, setting, and framework in which Bey2ollak thrived and became the success it is today.

The Story

He sits in a room full of young Egyptian men anxious to know their fate. Gamal—like many young Egyptian males—was selected to serve for a full year in the army. Some might think of this as a year to think about the future, to figure out what to do in life, or simply to shut one's brain off for a year and just follow orders. Others, like Gamal, decided to take advantage of it. He joined thousands, or rather millions, of Egyptians dreaming of becoming their own bosses and starting their own businesses. He wanted to become an entrepreneur.

Gamal was sharing his thoughts with his cousin Aly one evening, who for his part was rather unhappy with his corporate job. The two cousins decided to team up to create *something*. At that point, it wasn't yet clear what that something would be, but the idea of starting up their own business was there. Given their background and their computer science degrees, it was somewhat clear from the beginning that it was going to be a tech startup. Gamal was complaining about his mandatory military service, Aly was complaining about his corporate job, and all Egyptians were complaining about the traffic.

The People behind Bey2ollak
Soon enough, Gamal and Aly started taking action and talked to even more relatives to make their app come to life. They discussed this over their weekly Friday family lunch, which was nearly always preceded or accompanied by crazy traffic stories. Later on, four other friends joined the group to create a team of six ambitious entrepreneurs. Mohamed, Aly, and Gamal were responsible for the technical aspect of the application,

Fig. 2.1. New Bey2ollak users in 2013

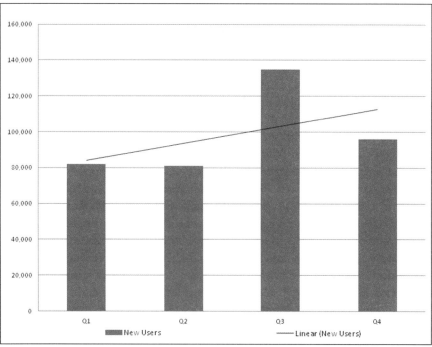

Source: These are numbers released exclusively for this case study. They have been directly obtained from the founders.

given their experience and their computer science degrees. Mostafa was in charge of the business angle, Yehia of the art direction, and Waleed was the operations manager. This dream team was the proud father of a new baby—Bey2ollak, which means 'it tells you' in Arabic.

Bey2ollak, simply put, is a crowdsourced traffic application for smartphones. All the roads of Greater Cairo and Alexandria can be rated based on the severity of traffic at any given point in time for others to see. Users create accounts and are then able to check their way to work and decide between alternative routes. Any user can update any given route with one of five levels of traffic flows that are marked by different colors as indicators: dark green, light green, yellow, orange, and red. Additionally, users can indicate if there is any danger, accident, construction, or simply ask a question. So far, Bey2ollak has been generating money through application sponsorship from Vodafone. Vodafone does not own the application; it is just the main sponsor. There are other sponsors, such as Pepsi and Shell. There is also some space for advertising. Bey2ollak now has an office in the Maadi area overlooking the Nile that houses about 25 employees.

The Environment
Bey2ollak's founders had observed that when someone arrived early to their weekly Friday lunch, they would call others to warn them of the jammed streets. They would also often see updates on Facebook, Twitter, or other social media warning friends and family away from taking certain roads because of accidents causing traffic or construction work creating a bottleneck. A World Bank study found that Egypt incurs about US$8 billion annually as an economic cost of traffic. Clearly there was a need for a unified platform for those traffic updates rather than depending on stumbling upon one on your way out of your office or en route to dinner with your friends.

Political Climate
The app kicked off on October 10, 2010, just three months before the Arab Spring hit Egypt in January 2011. For the most part, the app has grown and thrived in post-revolution Egypt. This alone increased the need for the app because demonstrations, roadblocks, and other unexpected events made rerouting essential on almost a daily basis. This was partly due to the expected congestion the aforementioned events were presumed to cause, but also due to the danger associated with coming close to demonstrations that could turn violent in the blink of an eye. This

new development on Egyptian streets was to the advantage of Bey2ollak, which provides real-time updates on all major routes in Greater Cairo. Aside from that, the nature of Egyptian streets also created a need for Bey2ollak. One broken-down Lada 128 is all it takes to bring the 6th of October bridge to a complete standstill, just as an accident on the Mehwar can block traffic both ways, and Downtown Cairo can become gridlocked all on its own. These, to mention a few, are occurrences that can make a five-minute car ride last for hours. Yet they don't always happen. Which means that taking a road always means not knowing if you will have a normal, twenty-minute drive or a three-hour traffic jam. Bey2ollak nearly eliminated this risk by giving people the ability to know the status of the road at any given point in time. The main advantage that Bey2ollak profited from is the very high degree of risk associated with the state of Egyptian streets. If the risk were smaller, the need for such an app would decline proportionally. If the situation were the same every single day, with traffic being a problem only during the morning and evening rush hours and all construction and renovation work announced beforehand, then Bey2ollak would not be as vital as it is today. The revolution also sparked a vibe of change that swept through the country, not only politically. Anything new and young had become more promising, setting the right conditions for new entrepreneurs.

Bey2ollak's team, quick to respond to changes on the Egyptian street, did another thing that was extremely smart and made yet another Cairene problem work for their benefit. When Egypt was repeatedly hit by fuel shortages, Bey2ollak immediately devoted a new section to fuel stations. Then came a couple of big election days and Bey2ollak struck again by creating sections for polling stations. Bey2ollak also helped to organize travel in convoys when it was unsafe to travel by road alone to the North Coast. The list goes on and on. It is a kind of symbiosis that has been created between Bey2ollak and Egypt—they work for each other's benefit.

Competitors

Yet another feature that has worked in Bey2ollak's favor, and perhaps the most essential, is the first-mover advantage. The first-mover advantage is a form of competitive advantage that a business has when it is the first to enter a market or an industry. This usually entails bringing a new, innovative product to the market that gains a lot of recognition and gets a big market share, which is the case of Bey2ollak. Many new traffic apps have entered the market, but have failed thus far to seize Bey2ollak's market share. Those other apps may or may not work better or have superior features, but they capitalized on what Bey2ollak had already started and it is difficult now to shift Bey2ollak's user base to those new entrants. Being the first to create a traffic app in this way and introducing it to Egypt has given Bey2ollak great brand recognition and customer loyalty that is unlikely to change in the near future. Competitors would need to exert a lot of effort to be able to achieve this shift, which could prove to be a bad idea. Bey2ollak's efforts toward user retention and the constant upgrading and development of the app are also making life difficult for competitors. Innovation has been essential for Bey2ollak from day one and will continue to be important. Otherwise, the risk of losing users will increase. For example, one of the new strong competitors is Taree2y, which has attracted more than 80,000 users in a short time. It follows the Bey2ollak model but differentiates its service by adding new, innovative features that detect the user's location and give directions to follow.

A Secondhand Culture

Some people claim that Egyptians were the first to start recycling. They were probably the first people to start reusing old glass Coca-Cola bottles for water, Nutella jars for homemade jams, old underwear as cleaning cloths, and so on. Egypt is a secondhand market. Cars get resold from user to user and never get 'thrown away' before they turn forty years, and a lot of the antique Mercedes and Peugeot cars that roam Cairo's streets daily can be seen on display in museums elsewhere. The same goes for the smartphone market. As a consequence, a large portion of the middle- to low-income class has access to expensive smartphones, thereby expanding the market that Bey2ollak is serving. It might not be the newest Samsung or iPhone, but it is definitely good enough to run Bey2ollak flawlessly. Bey2ollak first expected to serve a rather narrow social class aged between twenty-five and thirty-five. They were pleasantly surprised (and even more so as more time passed) that more and more people outside their initial target audience have been reached, not just in terms of social class but also in terms of age. The demographics of their target audience had been the typical twentysomething corporate-slave stereotype. But they later found fifty-year-old cab drivers asking their passengers to "check that thing on their phone" to see if the bridge is green. Of the user base, 13.8 percent is between 35 and 44, while 4.9 percent is between 45 and 55, and 3.5 percent is over 55. In addition to the secondhand-market aspect of the Egyptian market, the fact that smartphones from China (for example,

G–Tide) have flooded Abdel Aziz Street has also indirectly contributed to the widening of Bey2ollak's user base.

The app slowly but surely became an authority when it came to traffic in Egypt. Online news sites started citing Bey2ollak as a news source for events in the Egyptian streets. After all, it would be the fastest way to find out if anything were happening. The chances of a Bey2ollak user being present at the scene is higher than the chance of a news reporter being there. Bey2ollak created partnerships with radio stations and newspapers (such as *Shorouk* and *al-Watan*). This is yet another indicator of the success of the application. When a source is quoted multiple times in newspapers, it's a good sign of how credible it has become.

The Business Model

There are many great restaurants, amazing books, and plenty of outstanding apps out there that go unnoticed. On the other hand, things with little or no meaning or with a very low aesthetic value go viral and gain recognition from nearly every person on the planet. Thus, an app needs to be much more than just 'a good app' to make it big. It needs to be intriguing enough to go viral. Bey2ollak had that certain *je ne sais quoi* with its interesting personality, compelling logo design, and unusual use of Franco-Arabic language.

The app was neatly presented with a very catchy design and friendly user interface. On the first day it was available for download it just went *viral*. The launch targeted 1,000 users as a start; there were 6,000 registered users almost as soon as the application was launched.

This saved the team behind Bey2ollak a great deal of money in marketing, on top of the money they had saved by being a team with such diverse skills. The appealing logo alone had caught many an eye and attracted many users. Most importantly, Bey2ollak hit the jackpot with the choice of name. The name is an Egyptian way of expressing that you're about to say something you've heard somewhere by someone, with no specific source and of questionable reliability. This very local way of speech not only mirrors the nationality of the app (everything is 100 percent Egyptian), but it also brings Bey2ollak one step closer to its audience. The choice of the language, which is 'Franco-Arabic,' satisfied the needs of the target market by using their chatting language.

This brings us to the next favorable circumstance for Bey2ollak. Basically, they had everything they needed in their team. They had the designers, the business people, and the tech people. They also didn't need any advertising, as they used social media and their families and friends to spread the word. There was barely any start-up capital needed; all they needed to invest at first was their own time. This is a very important point, because probably the most common difficulty that startups face is very limited startup capital. But Bey2ollak's founders knew how to take advantage of every single resource they had, which ultimately led to their success. It goes without saying that things were also difficult. After all, they did not have much experience in the field. A lot of hard work was needed to make this work out for them as it did. But the bottom line remains: the app needed to go viral; it would be a hit or miss. It was a hit.

The Challenges

Success did not come to Bey2ollak on a silver platter, by any means. The risk they took was high. Would people care to update the routes? Why would they? If they did decide to update the route if it's blocked and they're stuck in their car and bored, would they bother if traffic is flowing just fine? People tend to complain about the bad more than they point out the good. Would that affect Bey2ollak? Maybe it's a crazy idea to depend on people so much? All these questions were carefully thought through, but nobody could give a definite answer. There was no similar model in the market to follow in terms of operation, or even an international benchmark since the environment in Cairo is unique and extremely challenging.

The founders did their homework by surveying people around them to obtain a rough estimate of how many would update the routes. They found that an estimated 10 percent of users would regularly update the routes. This means that if they needed 1,000 updates, 10,000 users would need to be registered. This was an eye-opening fact. A large user base was essential for the success of this business. Additionally, starting a business in the wake of a revolution cannot be easy for anyone. After a while, revenue needs to be generated and the company needs to grow. This was particularly important for the Bey2ollak group, as they were short of cash. The revolution has caused many investors—if not all—to have second thoughts about their investments. Attracting sponsors and advertisers took time due to the new nature of the business. With time it became a model by itself and the benchmark in the Egyptian market. This resulted in the emergence of new competitors, such as Taree2y, which differentiates itself by adding new, innovative features that do not rely on crowdsourcing but on GPS and Google Maps.

Concluding Remarks

It has to be said: luck was on Bey2ollak's side all along. External factors were in its favor from day one. Still, all the good luck in the world could not have made Bey2ollak the success it has become today. It has faced its fair share of challenges. The app industry is rarely marketed in the conventional ways. Thus, apps face a greater challenge in that area. They need to be good enough and have enough of a positive impact to spread through word of mouth alone. Constant upgrades and developments are also vital. Without them, decay would be inevitable. Moreover, the extreme risk associated with depending on users has not been easy on Bey2ollak. But as they say: the greater the risk, the greater the return.

Bey2ollak now boasts more than 1,000,000 registered users, 300,000 Facebook fans, and 130,000 Twitter followers. That is quite a success. The big questions remain, though: Has Bey2ollak found a universal recipe for success? How can they maintain their position in the market and differentiate themselves from emerging competitors with new features? What could be the next technological jump in order to attract more customers? Can they now spread their wings and expand into other markets, inside and outside of the Middle East?

References

World Bank. 2010. *Cairo Traffic Congestion Study.* Study, Economic and Sector Work, Cairo. Washington, DC: World Bank.

3 Adaptation and Business Model Innovation in Times of Rapid Change: Baraka Group Case Study

Ayman Ismail and Brendon Johnson

The revolution affected us positively," Ahmed Ragab explains, as he glances at the live video monitors of his new stores. "It forced us to rethink, to adapt, to move with the market."[1]
Ahmed Ragab is the current CEO of Baraka Group, a designer and importer of high-quality eyewear in Egypt. Growing from an importer and distributor of foreign goods, Baraka over the years has worked to differentiate itself as a niche brand of eyewear in Egypt. The company has refocused from offering exclusively high-market products to tapping an underserved youth demographic in Egypt. They have also become the first company in Egypt to design its own line of Egyptian-branded eyewear.

After the Egyptian revolution, sales dropped, stores were damaged, and celebrity endorsements were terminated. But while Baraka Group's competitors were struggling with instability—due to changing consumer habits, investors pulling out, and malls closing early—Ahmed and his team were designing creative strategies to adapt. It was around this time that Ahmed conceptualized and led the launch of the company's new 'pop-up' shop concept, a retail application adaptable to the movements and demands of an unstable market. This focus on leanness, efficiency, and an ability to quickly adjust to a changing market allowed Baraka Group to successfully grow in locations, sales, and profit in post-revolution Egypt.

A Business for Luxury Goods

Baraka Group, a family business, was established in 1979 by Mohamed Fathy Ragab and Ahmed Farid. Originally founded as a wholesale distributor for luxury goods, the company opened its first premium optical store in 1982. Based on a perceived 'market gap' for high-end eyewear in Egypt, the boutique was the first in the country to offer quality, fashionable, imported eyewear.

With a diverse product mix of foreign lines combined with an emphasis on customer service, Baraka Group soon became a trusted and well-established brand. For much of the 1980s and 1990s, the company acted as Egypt's sole distributor of high-quality foreign eyewear. But in the early 2000s, this market lead started to wane. As malls spread throughout Egypt and luxury goods became more readily available, competitors began to enter the market. To maintain a competitive edge, the co-founders recognized a need to adapt.

A Youthful Presence

In 2003, Mohamed Ragab and Ahmed Farid, seeking a new presence in their company, invited Mohamed's son Ahmed to join the company. Although as he was growing up it had always been presumed that Ahmed would eventually join the family business, in these years he had not been looking forward to joining Baraka. He was in his final year at the American University in Cairo studying political science and participating in a rotational program at Nike. "I enjoyed my job at Nike," Ahmed says, "and I wasn't quite ready to leave it."

Even though Ahmed knew that joining the family company was an inevitability, the idea of simply carrying the baton didn't appeal to him. In Egypt, Ahmed explains, the second generation is seen as the carriers of family businesses. The problem, he says, is that once they take over they try to change systems from within. But trying to restructure systems that have been implemented the same way for twenty to thirty years can prove a daunting task, often subject to failure.

Ahmed's new employers had a different vision for him, however. Rather than integrating him directly into current operations, they decided to give him the flexibility and space to develop new ideas by putting him at the forefront of a new, separate brand at the company. This new brand—C & Co.—would focus on a new market, and provide new, fresh opportunities for the company.

Filling a Gap

"Baraka Group's business model has always been about filling a gap," Ahmed says. In 1996, the family consortium became the first in Egypt to import luxury furniture. In 1999, the launch of Nike in Egypt offered the country's first branded sports product. And in 2001, Baraka became a first mover for high-end jewelry.

In the early 2000s, the co-founders isolated a gap in their offerings: young Egyptians were not purchasing their products. At that time, two markets existed for eyewear in Egypt. The first market comprised high-quality, high-priced imported glasses, while the second focused on lower-quality, lower-priced products. Baraka had a strong hold on the former for many years. These customers, primarily women and men between the ages of twenty-five and sixty, of middle- to upper-class economic status, would purchase two new pairs of eyeglasses per year at prices ranging from US$150 to US$500 per pair. The second market—young, price-conscious Egyptians—was instead dominated by these one-off neighborhood stores and street vendors. Most of the products offered at these stores were replicas, some vintage. Across the board, this eyewear had little uniqueness.

The Baraka team identified their missing target as youth with disposable income who sought imported and high-quality brands, but who couldn't afford or didn't want to pay for Baraka's luxury products. The Central Agency for Public Mobilization and Statistics (CAPMAS) notes that more than 60 percent of Egyptians are under thirty, with one-third of the country's total population under fifteen (CAPMAS 2014). Many of these young consumers will soon enter the workforce and thus build purchasing power. GDP per capita is predicted to rise by 63.9 percent by 2017, reaching US$4,500 over the same period and bringing millions of Egyptians into the middle class (*Egypt Retail Report* 2014). Meanwhile, per capita consumer spending in Egypt is forecast to increase by 72 percent by 2017, compared to a regional growth average of 47 percent (*Egypt Retail Report* 2014). With the rise of a middle class, demand for modern chain stores, which offer a wide array of options and discounts, is expected to rise in parallel.

Tapping this new market would require adaptation: with branding, products, locations, and the overall business model.

A More Colorful Brand

The new target client was identified as fashionable and hip, ranging in age from fifteen to thirty. They seek high-end and stylish yet affordable products. "Price is the main factor affecting their purchasing decision," Ahmed explains. Unlike Baraka's longstanding customer base, this demographic would seek products for their quality and their value.

In 2003, Ahmed joined the company, without a job description. He was responsible for leading market research, business and product design, and implementation for the company's new brand targeting this new youth demographic, C & Co. The eyeglasses they offered would continue to be high quality and imported, but at significantly lower prices. 'Colorful, youthful, and affordable' would be the key brand identifiers.

Baraka Optics launched the C & Co. brand in 2004. New shops were designed with a relaxed, youthful appeal, with coffee bars and lounge areas aimed at enhancing the customer experience. Creative promotions were developed to tailor to individual customers, making them feel special and unique. Sales staff was hired directly from the target market, ranging in age from eighteen to thirty. Many were recruited directly from universities, and the company even developed a structure offering students automatic vacations during university exam periods.

Over a period of twelve months, the company rapidly launched a series of eleven stores. "It was the shock strategy," Ahmed said. While this aggressive launch phase effectively doubled the overall operating budget of the brand (it wasn't until 2007 that C & Co. began to turn a profit), the strategy was effective in drawing the attention of new prospective customers.

An Egyptian Product Line

Even with the development of this new brand, Ahmed and the co-founders had noticed that Baraka's products were becoming increasingly less distinct from those of its competitors. Baraka Optics's traditional stores offer over sixty foreign brands. These are mainly from Europe and the United States, and include the likes of Bulgari, Chanel, Givenchy, Persol, and Ray-Ban. Although several exclusive partnerships between Baraka Group and foreign brands continued (and still do today)—making them available only in Baraka stores—in general Baraka eyewear was not much different from that of other high-quality eyewear companies.

The team thus conceptualized the idea of 'home brands.' These lines of higher-margin, innovative eyewear products would be designed and produced by the company to help differentiate it from competitors. Designed for the C & Co. line, brands would range from simple and classic, to fashionable and hip, to colorful and more economical. An in-house team of designers would develop the products, while Baraka Group contracted the production through foreign manufacturers. This would ensure uniqueness and high quality design while still offering international appeal.

Baraka Optics began designing the home brands and contracting with foreign entities in Italy, Greece, Japan, South Korea, and China. The Chinese-produced products would be lower-priced, while the higher-end brands would come from Europe and Japan and be made with premium quality materials. The products would range in price from US$40 to US$150.

By 2014, home brands had come to represent 35 percent of total sales generated. To illustrate a few: basic frames in the Blue-C line are made in China and cost an average of US$65, while the Squads line, made in Italy, features trendy eyewear at an average price of US$100.

Endeavoring Change

Ahmed stands up during an interview. "It helps me to walk around while talking," he says. Over the years, Ahmed tells me, he has become increasingly excited by his work in Baraka Group. The prospect of creating something new, and the challenge of trying something different, have together driven his ambition.

For the first three years, the C & Co. brand grew on average 50–60 percent annually. By 2007, the brand had stabilized and begun making a profit. In 2008, the team decided to merge C & Co. and Baraka Optics into one company.

But the next three years saw challenges. With the merging of two sets of staff, overhead grew at 70 percent, while revenues grew only at 20–25 percent. In particular, the company's wholesale business had been suffering a large loss. A currency depreciation in 2003 had increased supplier costs, negatively affecting the wholesale business's profitability. It had also been incurring a variety of unanticipated expenses. Meanwhile, other new brands that had recently been launched—such as Baraka People—were not performing nearly as well as the C & Co. brand.

Around this time, a friend of Ahmed's recommended he look at the Endeavor network for entrepreneurs. Endeavor's mission is to accelerate high-growth entrepreneurs, who are seen as catalyzers of long-term economic growth. Through mentoring support, technical assistance, and network access, Endeavor seeks to help high-potential entrepreneurs overcome barriers and achieve scale. In 2009, seeing the value of mentoring and network support to help him deal with his challenges, Ahmed applied to Endeavor Egypt. In 2010, Ahmed took part in the 37th International Selection Panel in

South Africa—a rigorous process consisting of a series of company reviews, interviews, and panels. The panel didn't select Baraka Group as an Endeavor company, but recommended that Ahmed first attempt to tackle a number of milestones, namely focusing product offerings, aligning commercial and financial performance, restructuring internally, and streamlining.

Revolutionary Times

Following the January 2011 revolution, Baraka experienced significant setbacks. In that year, sales dropped by US$12 million and three shops were damaged. The company had also just previously secured its first celebrity endorsement from the pop singer and actor Tamer Hosni. But Tamer Hosni's public support for the Mubarak regime during the revolution quickly ostracized him from the Egyptian public, and as a result Baraka terminated the partnership.

Tough times demand innovation. While the events in Egypt had hit companies hard, including Baraka's competitors, Ahmed felt as if it was a turn for the better. "When you're on the edge," he says, "you begin to make severe decisions you've been putting off for years." Based on the feedback of the original Endeavor committee, Ahmed had identified a need to refocus his company by concentrating exclusively on areas of strength and high profit. Too many directions and concepts had been creating confusion.

To start, Ahmed wanted to tackle wholesale. He felt that having their hands in both wholesale and retail was too much. The scale of wholesale—focused on obtaining and selling large quantities—contrasted with the smaller quantities required for retail operations. While wholesale had given Baraka control over the entire supply chain for years, it more recently had also limited their ability to control their own retail market.

The wholesale business had been a cornerstone of the company since its founding. Over the period of July 2010 through January 2011, Ahmed's father and uncle had invested a total of US$4.5 million to jolt the wholesale business. But now that the company simultaneously faced internal and external challenges, Ahmed saw an opportunity: to adapt to unstable conditions in an efficient way with the aim of increasing profitability. Well aware of the dynamics he was facing, Ahmed took advantage of Egypt's situation and argued that economic instability was only going to make the wholesale business suffer more. By refocusing the business on retail, where they would have stronger control over marketing and sales, they could increase profits. While it was challenging for the co-founders to relinquish their control over wholesale, they eventually agreed, and the wholesale business (as well as the unsuccessful spin-off Baraka People) was terminated.

Moving with the Crowd

Charged with this new prerogative of 'adaptation,' Ahmed began to look at how his company could be more flexible within the ever-changing political and economic conditions of his country. One way to adapt was to tackle directly the old fixed-location retail store model. Since everything—from politics, to investments, to customer habits—was becoming unpredictable, Ahmed saw fixed-location stores as too rigid of an investment.

For inspiration, Ahmed looked to the Egyptian street vendor. Selling produce from donkey-pulled carts, fruit juice from a portable stand, or ice cream from the back of a bicycle, street vendors, Ahmed notes, have one unique advantage: whenever the market changes, they can simply pick up and carry their products to a new location. "They move based on the crowd," Ahmed observes. As they are continually able to adapt to their customers' movements, their success is not contingent on location.

It was from here that Ahmed conceptualized the 'C & Co. Express' shop. A mobile pop-up shop, it was meant to be adaptable to a variety of venues, enabling the company to continually relocate based on market size, opportunity, and reliability. Designed to be constructed or dismantled in a matter of hours, the store could 'pop up' in a new spot at virtually any time. Once the sales and profit curve sloped down—if a market proved weak, maxed out after a period of time, or changed with the seasons—they could just pick up and leave. "It's like a shop as a backpack," Ahmed says.

Express shops were planned to be located in hot spots such as clubs, university campuses, and food plazas. Advantageously, these were locations with a limited number of physical stores, and thus competition for sales would be nearly nonexistent. An individual shop could move around throughout the year, remaining in one spot for as little as a few weeks or up to a few months. During the semester, an Express store might visit a series of universities, each for a few weeks at a time. Since customers generally would not change in these enclosed settings, after some time sales would max out, and the shop would then move on. They would target areas where customers would come and go on a regular basis, especially where they could purchase products directly related to their current situation and experience. For each location, the company would rent physical space for a designated period of time. Whenever the store wasn't in use, it would be stored in a special warehouse that the company rents for less than US$100 a month. And with the Express shop, there would be one simple rule: each store must generate a profit *immediately*. If this were not the case, the shop would be closed and its location reevaluated. The C & Co. Express shop was conceived by Ahmed in March 2011. That June, the first store was launched in a sports club in Zamalek, an affluent neighborhood of Cairo. In the first year, Express shops generated on average US$9,000 in monthly revenues per store.

An Egyptian Identity

New pricing strategies, an appeal to youth, and a collection of home brands were together beginning to differentiate Baraka from its competitors. But their products still primarily represented foreign styles. Even the home brands—designed by an Egyptian team—had little 'indigenousness' to them.

Just before the revolution, Baraka had conceived the launch of its first line of 'licensed' brands. Designed in collaboration with young local designers and public figures, the brands would build upon Egypt's artistic and cultural heritage to offer exclusive, Egyptian-branded eyewear. The products would offer something nobody else in Egypt was offering: eyewear with an Egyptian identity.

The first collection, Amina K. for Baraka Optics, was designed with inspiration from early Islamic art. The product prominently displayed the image of the Egyptian eagle. It sold out entirely in 2010. Following the revolution, Baraka Optics continued to commission Egyptian brands. Four additional product lines were launched under the Amina K. brand. A 2011 collaboration with M. Fares, a popular interior designer, created a second line (although this line was not continued due to a perceived lack of Egyptian uniqueness in the eyewear). Hebz, an Egyptian designer based in London, is currently partnering with Baraka to design an eyewear product blending Moroccan and Egyptian themes.

While the unrest in Egypt may have inspired more demand for Egyptian-branded products (Ahmed claims that if it had any impact on his market, it was minimal), it also caused occasional challenges. In particular, in 2012 Baraka developed a brand in partnership with the popular al-Ahly Football Club. Up until that point, football was one of the most popular activities in the country. Immediately before the launch of the products, however, violent football riots between teams at Port Said in northern Egypt had created a strong stigma attached to football teams across Egypt. Although the product line had been fully developed and produced, it was quickly liquidated.

Growth in a Receding Economy

While competitors were continuing to close shops by an estimated average of 20–30 percent, Baraka was expanding. From 2011 to 2013, the company launched twelve new Express shops, for a total of thirty-four stores across the country. While overall sales had dipped in 2011, net profit in the same period increased threefold to fourfold. Revenue stabilized at US$7.7 million.

In 2014, Baraka Group had 250 Egyptians employed across thirty-two retail outlets. On average, a C & Co. customer would purchase two or three pairs of eyeglasses per year. While C & Co. customers would spend on average $100 per purchase—less than the average spending of Baraka Optics—as of 2013, C & Co. stores had come to constitute 55 percent of Baraka Optics' total revenues. C & Co.'s profit margins grew from 5 percent in 2007 to 10–15 percent in 2014, and, Ahmed says, the business became more mature, with better output on marketing and sales. The company has also achieved greater control over its profit margin through licensed and house brands. While foreign imports only yield 30 percent average gross margins, house and licensed brands offer approximately 65 percent.

Ahmed was also formally accepted into the Endeavor network after participating as a comeback candidate in the 2013 International Selection Panel in Dubai. He has since received mentoring on issues of corporate governance, human resource management, growth strategy, and brand management, as well as jump-started the Baraka Optics Endeavor Advisory Board, which launched in the second quarter of 2014 with three high-profile members.

Adaptable and Market-driven

Through its Express outlets, the company is trying to reshape the retail industry, controlling all factors of operations including store dimensions, concept, location, and duration of operation. Baraka Group now has the flexibility and mobility to adapt and grow steadily under a variety of market conditions. In order to achieve the optimum operating model, they are experimenting with installation and reinstallation in different locations. Average monthly Express shop revenues have grown, from US$9,000 in 2011 to US$12,000 in 2014, with profit margins of 5–25 percent. Ahmed primarily attributes this growth to customer loyalty and trust. While overhead costs of Express shops actually match overheads of traditional stores (20 percent), Ahmed says the flexibility of the Express shop allows for more consistent profit generation.

One area of potential growth is through home and licensed brands. By developing and testing brands in their home country, Baraka is engaging directly with customers and designing products based on local tastes and desires. Ahmed sees a lot of potential here: the fact that Baraka is the only group creating new and *local* market trends can give the company a significant edge. The company plans to launch products by a new designer every year, as well as to continue new designs with previously contracted designers. There are challenges: Ahmed says designers in Egypt tend to be inconsistent, engaging with a short-term mindset and committing only to one-time designs rather than multi-year contracts. But Ahmed hopes that with growth in sales and opportunities, as well as a perceived rising interest in design careers in Egypt, Baraka can start to change this culture.

Meanwhile, with C & Co., Ahmed sees endless opportunities. Changes in demographics across Egypt are offering new opportunities, he says. As an increasing number of consumers are thinking with their pockets, rather than solely their fashion sense, Ahmed sees the potential to absorb more and more of this market share. "The target is very wide," he says, and his plans are to continue driving expansion by "covering all possible revenue-generating areas."

The company has positioned itself to reach US$14.6 million in revenue by the end of 2015. This will be primarily through expansion of new products and stores. The company plans to bring more Express stores to a wider range of spots such as universities and clubs.

Plans are also in the works for scaling regionally. Working partially through connections offered by Endeavor, the company has developed an agreement in the United Arab Emirates and hopes to enter the market in 2015. Regionally, though, Ahmed plans to move more slowly. While Baraka Group's research estimates that the market for high-end glasses and branded optical aids is more than US$2.1 billion in the region (specifically in the Gulf Cooperation Council countries), very little information is available on the potential for non-luxury goods offered by the C & Co. concept. Ahmed believes this market to be young and promising, but he is approaching the region cautiously. "It's very risky not to be profitable outside of Egypt," he says, "where it is more difficult to fix problems." Just like with the launch of the C & Co. brand in Egypt, they plan to calculate every step.

The challenges faced by competitors during the recession have essentially given Baraka market dominance. Following the launch of C & Co., most of Baraka's competitors tried to capture a portion of this new market by launching their own new brands targeting youth. But after one to two years, each ended up shutting down these new brands, ranging from two to five shops per competitor. The difference, Ahmed observes, is that competitors "just thought they needed to create another brand, rather than an entire new concept." The C & Co. concept, from day one, worked on developing an entirely new strategy: from product, to structure, to sales. "It involved a lot of homework," he says.

If Baraka doesn't continue to adapt, though, that market lead might not last long. Ahmed has a vision to make Egyptian-branded eyewear a regionally coveted accessory. To stay ahead of the curve, Ahmed believes the company must be able to constantly reevaluate. The key, according to him, is to launch a new business line every three to four years. In 2007, the new line was C & Co. In 2011, it was Express. "In 2015," he says, "something big will happen." He's not exactly sure what yet, but whatever it is, it will aim to fill the market gap with innovation.

Notes

1   This case study was developed in collaboration with Endeavor Egypt. Endeavor is a global nonprofit organization whose mission is to catalyze long-term economic growth by selecting, mentoring, and accelerating the best high-impact entrepreneurs around the world.

References

"Baraka Group Entrepreneur Profile." 2014. Cairo: Endeavor Group.
Central Agency for Public Mobilization and Statistics (CAPMAS). 2014. Egypt in Figures. http://www.capmas.gov.eg
Egypt Retail Report. 2014. Business Monitor International.
Euromonitor International. 2010. Consumer lifestyles in Egypt. http://www.euromonitor.com

4 ChoCo'a: Growth Strategy for an Established SME

Sanjai K. Parahoo and Ashraf A. Mahate

Prologue

As Assem Hamzeh reached his office early on a pleasant winter morning in February 2014, he was thoughtful. As managing director of ChoCo'a, he was about to meet with the senior executive team to present a new set of strategies that he had been working on to take the company into the next phase of its growth and global expansion. With the unflinching support of his wife Dina, Assem had led ChoCo'a through the initial phase of start-up, growth, and stabilization so that their new entrepreneurial venture was now well-established in the UAE market. Assem received various accolades from friends and customers on this achievement. There comes a time, however, when a company must assume new challenges to sustain its growth potential. And he thought it was time ChoCo'a developed strategies to achieve the next phase of its growth, which would imply steering the ship into deeper and more turbulent waters and overcoming more formidable challenges. This was precisely the objective of his presentation, a task that had taken the best part of his time in the preceding few months. He was keen to present his thoughts on how ChoCo'a should develop specific strategies and action plans to build on its successful first decade in business and its core values. As he switched on his laptop to finalize his presentation, his thoughts wandered temporarily.

It was less than ten years ago! Assem remembered how he and Dina had achieved their professional dream in setting up their own chocolate boutique, aptly named ChoCo'a, in Dubai in 2004 (see fig. 4.1). Their passion for chocolate was their driving force. In Dina's words: "We use only the finest ingredients to produce the crème de la crème of the chocolate world. ChoCo'a has an extremely dedicated team, and our strength lies in the attention to the smallest details to ensure a chocolate experience as exceptional as one could really savor."

ChoCo'a Company History

Choco'a (http://www.chocoa.ae/) is a UAE-based limited liability company owned by Dina and Assem Hamzeh. Assem is the managing director and manages the entire operation and development of ChoCo'a. Dina is the retail director, responsible for executing and maintaining strategy, process, and development of the single ChoCo'a boutique store in Dubai.

The involvement of Assem and Dina in the chocolate industry can actually be traced back to two decades ago. Assem was a professional in the advertising agency in his native Lebanon, and one of his main accounts was a chocolate company, which was seeking to substantially grow its market presence. The company approached Assem to play a key role in guiding it through the next phase of its growth. Assem decided to take up the challenge. In the next decade, he steadily and confidently acquired considerable hands-on experience and expertise in the various processes involved in chocolate manufacturing and of the major stakeholders in the chocolate industry generally. When the same chocolate company wanted to grow its presence in regional markets by setting up a chocolate factory in Saudi Arabia, Assem was offered the position of assistant general manager in the plant. A sense of adventure and risk-taking combined with his innate self-belief led Assem to take up the challenge, leaving his comfortable and stable job in Lebanon to move to Saudi Arabia.

After nine months in Saudi Arabia, Assem felt homesick as the visa procedures for his family were dragging on. Finally, tired of waiting for the visas that would allow his family to join him in Saudi Arabia, Assem consulted with his family and took the drastic decision to leave his production manager position in Saudi Arabia and return to Lebanon. Although Assem did not have a clear business plan for the future, he was armed with determination. His strong understanding of the various stages of chocolate manufacturing, combined with his innate passion, had ignited his interest in pursuing entrepreneurial opportunities in the chocolate industry.

Fig. 4.1: Dina and Assem Hamzeh in the ChoCo'a Boutique

ChoCo'a: From Concept to Market Launch

Upon Assem's return to Lebanon, it was business incubation time, when Assem and Dina developed the foundation of the concept behind their new venture. They mixed chocolate ingredients at home, experimented with new ingredients, and did trials of variances in the manufacturing processes. From this early time, Assem was convinced that chocolate needed to be "respected," with its consumption being an "educational experience." With the help of some close friends who provided creative advice, the concept was refined and the brand name ChoCo'a was coined, as a creative combination of the French word *chocolat* and 'cocoa.' They selected an artistic depiction of a cocoa leaf as their logo which was combined with the slogan 'spread the obsession.' As seen in figure 4.2, the brand name vividly illustrates the admiration of the owners not only for a key source of quality chocolate but also the passion required to make quality chocolate. This philosophy is expressed in the words of Dina: "We believe that it is not only the cocoa beans, but passion, which makes great chocolate."

Fig. 4.2. Brand name, logo, and tagline of ChoCo'a

The husband and wife team developed ChoCo'a as a unique concept and a 'one-stop shop' as it grouped the finest from a variety of products, a concept that is still quite unique in the UAE. They opted to import the highest quality couverture chocolate from Belgium, an important reference for chocolate, and recruited international, experienced chefs with strong expertise. The chefs were encouraged to mix the base ingredients creatively with premium, innovative Oriental and Occidental flavors to create the mouth-watering confectioneries that ChoCo'a is known for.

Production is undertaken in a modern factory with the highest standards of safety and hygiene and a strict adherence to international standards of quality (see fig. 4.3). This commitment of ChoCo'a to quality and food safety led the firm to seek and achieve Hazard Analysis Critical Control Point (HACCP) certification from the British Standards Institution in 2007.

ChoCo'a thus grew into a manufacturer and retailer of chocolate products with a passion to 'provide exquisite chocolate.' The product range of ChoCo'a extends from an assortment of exclusive pastries and cakes to custom arrangements and specially designed cakes for all occasions and celebrations. ChoCo'a also specializes in custom-made corporate products for companies seeking their very own branded chocolate gifts. Interestingly, the company has also created a special sugar-free collection to cater to customers who wish to indulge in its scrumptious offerings without the guilt. While the factory includes state-of-the-art automated machines for mass production, Assem has developed parallel artisan production processes that retain a strong element of artistic craftsmanship. The craft production enables ChoCo'a to offer flexibility and creativity in its products and to customize orders to individual customer needs.

Fig. 4.3: ChoCo'a factory outlet uses automation for highest quality and hygiene standards

Fig. 4.4: A view of the ChoCo'a Boutique in Al Barsha in Dubai

The management of ChoCo'a selected Dubai for its location, linking the positive image of the city relating to 'distinction,' 'indulgence,' and 'superiority' with its own brand positioning. In 2004, Assem selected a location in the Al Barsha area for its retail outlet (see fig. 4.4), a visionary decision as the area later developed into a prime commercial area with the opening of the imposing Mall of the Emirates in September 2005. The ChoCo'a outlet—or boutique, as it is aptly called—is an intricately and artistically designed display area of 200 square meters, with a large counter area for retail customers.

Background: Global and Regional Chocolate Industry

Chocolate is a processed product derived from the fruit of the cacao tree and is used in various types of confectioneries. Its story dates back to ancient times, starting a little over 3,000 ago in ancient South and Central American civilizations (The Chocolate Review, 2014). Both the Aztecs and the Mayans concocted a foamy drink with cacao, and spiced it with chili, honey, or vanilla, with the beverage enjoyed mostly by the elite upper class as it was an expensive luxury. Cacao beans were first discovered by Christopher Columbus in Guanaja in Honduras in 1502 (*The Chocolate Review*, 2014). It was taken to Europe in the early 1600s by the Spanish, who learned about it from the Aztecs (Powis, Hurst, Rodríguez, Ortíz, Blake, Cheetham, Coe, and Hodgson 2007).

Chocolate became popular initially among affluent Europeans, leading to the establishment of fashionable chocolate houses in large cities in Europe during the seventeenth century (AESSEAL 2003). In 1847, Joseph Fry discovered that by blending a little cocoa butter with chocolate liquor and sugar, a solid eating chocolate could be formed, and this led to the birth of the chocolate bar (AESSEAL 2003). In 1922, a malted milk bar with a chocolate covering was developed by Frank Mars, leading to the Mars bar; this innovation led to the development of the soft-center chocolate confectionery industry (AESSEAL 2003).

Building on these early innovations and widespread, blissful consumer adoption of chocolate over the past century, the economic significance of contemporary chocolate markets has become indisputable (Zarantonello and Luomala, 2011). In terms of net sales, the major global confectionery companies are based primarily in the United States, Switzerland, and Japan (see table 4.1). Global revenues from the chocolate industry are on the rise, with a predicted annualized growth of around 2 percent over the period 2012–17 (KPMG 2012).

Table 4.1. Global confectionary companies that manufacture some form of chocolate, by net confectionery sales value in 2013

Company	Net sales 2013 (US$ billion)
Mars, Inc. (USA)	17.6
Mondelēz International, Inc. (USA)	14.9
Nestlé SA (Switzerland)	11.8
Meiji Holdings Co. Ltd. (Japan)	11.7
Ferrero Group (Italy)	10.9
Hershey Foods Corp. (USA)	7.0
Arcor (Argentina)	3.7
Chocoladenfabriken Lindt & Sprüngli AG (Switzerland)	3.1
Ezaki Glico Co. Ltd. (Japan)	3.0
Yildiz Holding (Turkey)	2.5

In the UAE, the growth has proved to be even steeper, with chocolate confectionery displaying a current value growth of 7 percent in 2012, to reach AED829 million (US$226 million). In the UAE market, Mars GCC remained the undisputed leader in chocolate confectionery with a value share of 42 percent in 2012, supported by brands such as Galaxy, Snickers, Twix, Mars, and M&M's. The second position was occupied by Nestlé Middle East FZE, with a retail value share of 17 percent for 2012, supported largely by the strong position of the KitKat brand (Euromonitor 2013).

Chocolate is increasingly a premium product, with brands such as Godiva and Lindt becoming almost mass market as consumers develop a taste for everyday glamour (KPMG 2012). In the UAE this phenomenon has been particularly noticeable with the emergence of artisan chocolatier brands that are positioned to serve this luxury-seeking customer segment. The 2013 figures from Euromonitor for the UAE indicate that total sales of various types of chocolates in 2012 amounted to AED1.739 million, of which no less than 48 percent represented sales of confectioneries (see table 4.2). Therefore, the segment of chocolate confectioneries targeted by the artisan chocolatiers is by no means small, although the local artisan brands do face stiff competition from global giants such as Mars and Nestlé. As in all asymmetrical battles, the underdogs have some attributes.

These may be identified as being a small, local company, appealing owner stories, market proximity, and a better appreciation of customer needs that they may leverage in their favor.

Table 4.2. Sales of chocolate confectionery by category in the UAE: Value in AED millions, 2007–12

	2007	2008	2009	2010	2011	2012
Alfajores/Bagged selflines/softlines	29.0	33.5	37.5	41.9	46.3	51.1
Boxed assortments	46.2	53.3	58.4	64.5	71.9	80.9
Standard boxed assortments	32.7	37.6	41.1	45.3	50.9	58.2
Twist-wrapped miniatures	13.5	15.7	17.3	19.3	20.9	22.7
Chocolate with toys	2.4	2.8	3.1	3.4	3.7	4.0
Countlines	261.2	303.7	334.4	364.1	393.4	415.8
Seasonal chocolate tablets	174.1	201.7	224.1	243.9	260.4	277.1
Chocolate confectionery	512.8	595.1	657.5	717.8	775.7	828.9

Source: Euromonitor, 2013

In the UAE, although the chocolate industry is comparatively small, there are about eighteen chocolate factories in Dubai alone (ChoCo'a internal document). As with many food products in the UAE, several chocolatiers in the UAE import ready-made confectionery products from countries such as Belgium, France, or Switzerland and place their own brand on the products (ChoCo'a internal document). As mentioned by KPMG (2012), an interesting development over the past decade has been the emergence of a 'luxury' category, which constitutes the prime target market of ChoCo'a.

ChoCo'a: Marketing Mix Considerations
Product mix decisions for its target markets
ChoCo'a has chosen to market its broad range of products using the unique company brand name (fig. 4.5). The company has in-house research and development personnel and designers who create chocolate gifts and special arrangements, resulting in a dynamic product range responding to the needs of consumer and business markets (see table 4.3 for details).

Fig. 4.5. A sample of ChoCo'a's chocolate confectioneries

1. Retail customer over-the-counter sales (consumer markets, B2C)
   - Boutique chocolate (assortments of retail chocolates, pre-packed collections, and boules glacées, macarons, and flavored confectioneries)
   - Chocolate arrangements (for various occasions including weddings, births, and festivities such as Ramadan, Eid, or Christmas)
   - Boutique cakes (exclusive cakes shaped in distinctive designs)
   - Specialty cakes and decorated items (for weddings, special designs for kids, birthday and corporate designs)
2. Corporate sales (business markets, B2B)
   - Corporate and private labels (tailor-made chocolate items wrapped according to corporate specifications)
   - Foods and beverages (F&B) for hotels, coffee shops, and restaurants

As mentioned previously, ChoCo'a has identified eighteen chocolate factories in Dubai alone. Most of these serve the retail market, providing local products or imported global brands. In a city renowned for its sweet tooth, ChoCo'a has a host of competitors in the chocolate retail market including Godiva, Hershey's, Forey & Galland, La maison du chocolat, Patchi, and Bateel.[1] Some of these brands, such as Patchi and Bateel, have also established themselves in the corporate market as strong competitors to ChoCo'a.

The chocolate market in Dubai is therefore diversified and fragmented (see table 4.4 below). While the major global brands capture the lion's share of the confectionery market, there is scope for artisan retailers to differentiate themselves as they serve three market segments (retail dine-in, retail walk-in, and corporate customers). This raises the question: why

Table 4.3. Product/target market mix for retail and corporate customers of ChoCo'a

	Market segment	Products/services	Outlet and channel
1	Customers: Retail counter	Various product assortments: chocolates, cakes, tarts, French patisserie, and pastries; pre-packed boxed chocolate gifts of various milk or dark chocolates (Arabian Delights, Oriental Delights, and mixed) in creative designs for events such as weddings, new babies, festivals, and birthdays. In-house designers to custom-design clients' orders	Counter sales in shop at Al Barsha
2	Corporate: Businesses and F&B sector	In addition to its wide range of boxed gift products, the creative designers of ChoCo'a create chocolate gifts and special arrangements to corporate requirements. ChoCo'a targets hospitality industries (F&B) for rooms and banquet services. It also serves corporate businesses including airlines, providing private label brands on boxed confectioneries to enhance corporate identity.	Delivery to premises

would a retail customer buy the more expensive and less convenient artisanal brand as opposed to to the global confectionery brands?

Before responding to this question, it would be useful to take a close look at the psychology of consumer behavior, which reveals three distinct types of buyers, each with different behaviors and demands (KPMG 2012):

1. *The convenience buyer.* Although chocolate is often considered an impulse purchase, it is increasingly a planned purchase. Convenience is becoming more important to time-stressed shoppers, so that the sale of tablet bars is becoming a lucrative market. A desire for convenience is also increasing the popularity of sharing bags, as consumers buy to share or finish eating later, characterized by the 'memory wrapper' from Mars that allows bars to be twisted, closed, and saved.

2. *The value buyer.* Value is an important consideration in many markets, particularly where the middle class is still being defined. For example, in the

United States, 79 percent of consumers look for good value when purchasing chocolate, although 70 percent also want a name brand, implying that even value shoppers are expecting the reassurance of a quality brand.
3. *The luxury buyer.* With an increasing number of customers in both developing and developed economies adopting the premise that expensive chocolate is an affordable luxury, the luxury chocolate market is embracing the mainstream. After the global financial crisis, there has been a quest by consumers for value, but also for products that exceed their expectations.

In such a market environment, "consumers like artisan companies because they are high quality and unique and that uniqueness and independence must remain" (KPMG 2012). The changing consumer behavior trends may represent a competitive advantage for artisan chocolatiers. For this they must leverage their uniqueness, local roots, fresh ingredients, and responsiveness to customer needs and the latter's specific local tastes and preferences to establish linkages with the customers. In so doing, artisan chocolatiers increase their potential to deliver product mix offerings that represent value to all three types of buyers described above. For example, convenience may be achieved by offering desired portion sizes with packaging adapted to the climate; value may be offered through the reassurance and affinity developed with a well-recognized local brand; luxury may be realized through specific design creations to match the local mood, festivities, and events. In this endeavor, the local chocolatier artisans benefit from appealing personal owner stories. The challenge for local artisan chocolatiers is to achieve differentiation of their own brands in a highly competitive market while vying against global rivals with superior advertising muscles and a global brand identity.

For a boutique chocolatier such as ChoCo'a, this implies careful positioning in its target markets. This is a particularly tricky issue, for the different segments have different needs and aspirations. For example, the retail luxury customers are looking for that special product that is different from those of global commercial brands targeted to mass markets. Yet these retail customers, many from a growing middle class, are also looking for value (KPMG 2012). ChoCo'a must therefore strive to deliver value to this segment to lure them away from generic mass outlets, such as supermarkets, that offer global chocolate brands. This has led ChoCo'a to position its products as an 'affordable luxury.' The objective is to enable ChoCo'a to increase the percentage retail sales value of specialist chocolate confectioners beyond the current value of 13.5 percent (table 4.4). On the other hand, corporate customers are looking for an exclusive brand with a luxury and high-end image that will enhance their own corporate brand when they associate with it and offer it as a corporate gift. Finally, in the case of ChoCo'a, there is an untapped segment of retail dine-in customers who are looking for indulgence in an exclusive ambience to unwind and socialize with friends. In the next section, the needs of this segment and how they may best be served are discussed.

Table 4.4. Chocolate confectionery company market shares in the UAE, 2008–12

	2008	2009	2010	2011	2012
Mars GCC	38.8	38.6	40.1	41.1	41.7
Nestlé Middle East FZE	15.9	16.0	16.6	17.1	16.8
Kraft Food Dubai	5.4	6.5	7.3	8.4	8.8
Cadbury Middle East FZE	7.1	5.7	6.3	6.5	7.1
Hershey Co.	2.6	2.8	4.4	5.1	5.6
Lindt & Sprüngli AG	4.4	3.1	2.8	2.4	2.2
Nestlé SA	1.8	1.8	1.8	1.9	2.1
Ferrero SpA	1.7	1.8	1.7	1.7	1.7
Storck August GmbH	0.5	0.5	0.5	0.5	0.5
Others	21.8	23.1	18.6	15.4	13.5
Total	100.0	100.0	100.0	100.0	100.0

Source: Euromonitor, 2013

Distribution channel considerations

Retail outlets for chocolate are numerous and diverse in Dubai. Hypermarkets and supermarkets are expected to retain the bulk share of chocolate confectionery sales from 2012 to 2017, however (Euromonitor 2013). Figure 4.6 shows the global chocolate retailers' market share (Euromonitor 2011, cited by KPMG 2012). (Supermarkets and discount stores account for 45 percent of global total sales of chocolate confectioneries in 2011, while specialist stores account for a mere 10 percent. With the entry of small supermarkets that are being constructed in growing residential areas in Dubai, it is expected that these will see stronger growth (from 28 percent share currently) than hypermarkets, which will see their market share remain effectively static at 53 percent of retail sales (Euromonitor 2013).

Fig. 4.6. Global chocolate retailers' market share

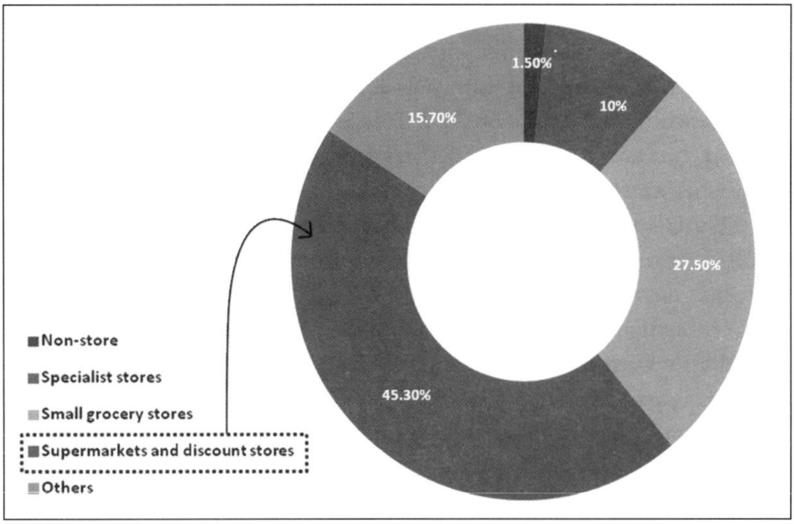

Source: Euromonitor 2011, cited by KPMG 2012

This trend has major implications for chocolate artisans. Although chocolate may be seen as an impulse purchase, it is increasingly becoming a regular habit among customers who therefore seek convenience in their purchases (Euromonitor 2013). Many retail customers seek to purchase chocolate to share or finish eating later, and this calls for packaging or wrapping that enables and facilitates this consumer behavior. Chocolate artisans need to be aware of this trend. Of course in Dubai the heat is a factor, and artisan chocolatiers such as ChoCo'a must take this into account in their packaging of retail sales.

Weather conditions in Dubai encourage residents to socialize in air-conditioned malls, and the cultural habit of indulgence through consumption of luxury non-alcoholic beverages is prevalent. This represents an opportunity for up-market, cozy, dine-in chocolate outlets to offer a response to customers looking for indulgence and luxury well beyond what coffee franchises (for example, Starbucks, Costa, Tim Hortons, and so on) have to offer. The dine-in chocolate market is currently served by brands such as Alison Nelson chocolate bar, Bateel café, and Vintage chocolate lounge, among others. As part of its growth strategy, ChoCo'a envisages a presence in the dine-in market as well.

In addition to its offers to retail customers and corporates, ChoCo'a plans to develop a ChoCo'a dine-in boutique, which will be distinct from their Al Barsha outlet. It will involve a chocolate bar with a comfortable seating area to act as a perfect sanctuary for those who wish to unwind while treating themselves to the finest selection of chocolates and pastries, while being pampered by high-level personalized service. Dina explains her philosophy: "Our objective is to encourage clients to think of ChoCo'a as a well-deserved treat for themselves and their loved ones and not only for gifts on personal or corporate occasions." Since the dine-in customers are looking for indulgence in an exclusive atmosphere with a pampering service, ChoCo'a has decided to open its retail outlet in a separate location. The retail dine-in concept and mode of market entry (outlets fully owned by ChoCo'a, franchising, or developing strategic alliances with external partners) will require careful elaboration (see table 4.5).

Table 4.5. The proposed product/market mix for ChoCo'a dine-in customers

Market segment	Products/services	Outlet and channel
Dine-in customers, primarily female 25–50 years: locals, Arab expatriates, GCC and MENA residents, with Western and Asian expats representing a growth market	Chocolate drinks Chocolate confectioneries, cakes, tarts, and pastries	New concept under development: chocolate bar to act as a sanctuary to unwind with high-level personalized service

Source: Internal Choco'a company document

Internal ChoCo'a company research and knowledge of the market has shown that the prime target market for a chocolate dine-in outlet remains a female segment, which currently represents the mass of actual customers. Typically, chocolate bars represent socialization with family and friends and are favored by locals and Arab expatriates, as well as GCC (Gulf Cooperation Countries) and MENA (Middle East and North Africa) visitors. There is a growing market for the service among Western and Asian expats.

Like many modern companies, ChoCo'a has embraced e-commerce. Since March 2012, it has been selling goods on its website (http://www.e-chocoa.com/), where a user-friendly interface and an attractive design enable customers to select from a product range beautifully illustrated with professional images and place their order at the convenience of a click.

Promotion mix

Like many entrepreneurial ventures, ChoCo'a has focused on promotional activities that provide efficient returns on investments. ChoCo'a has thus been actively involved in promotional activities in synergy with strategic partners. This has involved setting up demonstration booths in famous malls in Dubai in joint marketing efforts with an upmarket French department store located in Dubai. Visitors could thus have the opportunity to be immersed in a chocolate experience, smell the aroma of fresh chocolate being molded into delectable products by expert chocolatiers and designers, and sample the products. ChoCo'a has partnered with a major global automobile brand that has a compatible image of luxury and exclusiveness in an event to launch a new car model. It has also promoted its products in a tie-in through activities organized by an exclusive club of residents.

Such activities have helped ChoCo'a interact with its customers, educate them about its brand identity and its chocolate products, and obtain their feedback and taste preferences. This interaction is further enhanced by continuous communication through its dynamic Facebook account (https://www.facebook.com/chocoachocolate), where ChoCo'a reached the landmark of 6,000 likes in February 2014, a milestone celebrated with promotional activities.

While continuing to develop its share of chocolate products and services in the competitive local market, the company has decided to internationalize, by partnering with gourmet stores in countries such as Russia, Japan, Australia, Morocco, Bahrain, Saudi Arabia, Kuwait, and Lebanon to expand the international distribution of its products. ChoCo'a professes a future strategy to expand to other international markets. To support its export strategy and promote its brand, the company has participated in prestigious global exhibitions and fairs.

Pricing Decisions

The pricing of ChoCo'a reflects the quality of its ingredients and the exclusivity of hand-made designer products. Nonetheless, ChoCo'a has developed a diverse product mix, with prices of its product lines ranging from market penetration prices for its basic mass products to market skimming for its exclusive designer creations. While retaining its luxury image, its objective is to represent 'affordable luxury' to a growing market of retail customers.

As an illustration, for their Ramadan collection, the prices proposed by ChoCo'a for off-the-shelf creations varied from AED300–400 for the more exclusive arrangements to AED40–120 for smaller, less elaborate

chocolate boxes. The various competitors in the chocolate retail industry in Dubai emphasize differentiation in their individual creations rather
than attempting to compete on price. As a result, it is not possible to make
like comparisons based on price. Nevertheless, an online comparison of
prices per unit mass of competing creations for festivals between ChoCo'a
and global competitors such as Patchi and Godiva showed that the price
ranges were generally comparable. This rules out price as a differentiator in
customer purchase decisions, implying that customer choice hinges on the
extent to which the competitors meet customer needs and the strength of
the competitors' respective brand images.

People Dimension

As in all service industries, the involvement of the service personnel is
critical to delivering a great customer experience (Lovelock 2011). To this
end, ChoCo'a has availed itself of the services of international experienced chefs who have stayed with the company for years, enabling them
to combine their knowledge of international chocolate-making with local
taste preferences and customs and create unique products adapted to the
UAE and regional market.

A visitor to the factory can meet the team of nearly 75 employees of
different nationalities, all sharing the vision of the founders and operating in a family atmosphere. The work culture and environment exude a
positive ambience, which transfers to the products that come out of the
production line.

Epilogue

The jingle of the meeting reminder on his laptop drew Assem Hamzeh
back to the present. He cast a glance at his cue cards that would guide him
in defining the growth and expansion strategies to respond to the opportunities and threats facing ChoCo'a and reminded himself of the main
points of his presentation:

1. Consolidate the brand image and positioning of ChoCo'a as a local and
   regional artisan chocolatier by developing a communications strategy to:
   a. Grow its share of the local retail chocolate market, particularly vis-à-
      vis global confectionery brands
   b. Grow its share of the regional retail chocolate market, particularly
      vis-à-vis global confectionery brands
   c. Grow the presence of ChoCo'a in the corporate chocolate market

2. Affect the entry of ChoCo'a in the Dubai dine-in chocolate market to:
   a. Grow the turnover of the company
   b. Consolidate the brand image and positioning of ChoCo'a as a local/regional chocolate artisan.

As Assem walked purposefully toward the committee room, glancing at his presentation entitled "A Growth Strategy for ChoCo'a," he smiled, confident that he had come up with a viable plan for a bright future for ChoCo'a.

Notes

1 http://www.thedubaimall.com/en/shop/chocolates_confectionary_ice_cream/

References

AESSEAL. 2003. "Guide to Sealing the Chocolate Confectionery Industry." http://www.arthomson.com/Literature/brochures/MechSeals/AESSEAL/IndustrySealingGuides/L_UK_CHOC.pdf.

Euromonitor International. 2013. *Passport: Chocolate confectionery in the United Arab Emirates.* January.

"The History of Chocolate." 2014. *The Chocolate Review.* http://thechocolatereview.com/history-of-chocolate/the-history-of-chocolate.html

KPMG. 2012. "The Chocolate of Tomorrow: What Today's Market Can Tell Us about the Future." June.

Lovelock, C., and J. Wirtz. 2011. *Services Marketing: People, Technology, Strategy.* 7th ed. Upper Saddle River, NJ: Prentice Hall.

Martin, D.M. 2009. "The Entrepreneurial Marketing Mix." *Qualitative Market Research: An International Journal* 12, no. 4: 391–403.

Powis, Terry G., W. Jeffrey Hurst, María Del Carmen Rodríguez, Ponciano C. Ortíz, Michael Blake, David Cheetham, Michael D. Coe, and John G. Hodgson. 2007. "Oldest Chocolate in the New World." *Antiquity* 81, no. 314. http://www.antiquity.ac.uk/projgall/powis/index.html

Zanetos Scully, C. 2014. "2014 Global Top 100: Candy Industry's Exclusive List of the Top 100 Confectionery Companies in the World!" *Candy Industry*, 31 January. http://www.candyindustry.com/articles/86039-global-top-100-candy-industrys-exclusive-list-of-the-top-100-confectionery-companies-in-the-world?page=5

Zarantonello, L., and H.T. Luomala. 2011. "Dear Mr Chocolate: Constructing a Typology of Contextualized Chocolate Consumption Experiences through Qualitative Diary Research." *Qualitative Market Research: An International Journal* 14, no. 1: 55–82.

5 Funlozia's Dune Raider Befriends the Egyptian Desert Sands

Iman Seoudi and Mirette Shoeir

On a sunny afternoon in November 2013, the three partners of Funlozia sat together sipping their cups of coffee and contemplating the strategic redirection that lay ahead of them. Karim Hossam looked at the reassuring face of Mohamed Fadly, and noticed the sparkle of excitement that shone in the eyes of Mohamed Elwan, and he suddenly felt a rush of gratitude for having such committed partners at the helm of Funlozia. True, things weren't always pretty between the partners; time and again the office bore witness to grueling arguments among the top management team on one issue or another. Many bleak moments had overwhelmed the trio and threatened looming disaster. Every time they came through, though, and their company, partnership, and friendship grew stronger with every challenge. This was yet another challenge and Karim's gut feeling told him the three musketeers would see it through, just as they had many times before. Karim broke the silence.

"Dune Raider will turn sandboarding in Egypt from a hobby into a professional sport and leave competitors behind. We will host the 2015 International Sandboarding Tournament and invite Erik Johnson, the 2013 world champion. Let our copycats try to mimic this one!"

"Do you think Erik Johnson will be willing to come to Egypt, given the political conditions and the fledgling state of sandboarding in this country?" ventured Elwan.

"He's actually quite excited about it!" Karim responded, seeming unconcerned.

"And those customers who join our sandboarding trips and are serious about sandboarding can join our future professional sandboarding. It's a whole new ball game!" Fadly beamed.

A fresh positioning strategy for Dune Raider was only one item on the Funlozia top management team's agenda that afternoon. There were a host of other important strategic issues to be discussed. Competitors had entered the sandboarding market and were claiming that they were the first to introduce the sport in Egypt. In the corporate segment, the company's Go Camp team-building service was competing with large, established companies that have higher brand awareness, but who are not nearly as creative as Funlozia. The team needed to strengthen their presence in the market for overnight adventure camping by further building up their third branded line, Camponita. With a dynamic and rapidly expanding company on their hands, it was often challenging for the trio to get strategy right and to set priorities among the three rising brands. Coordinating everything that was happening in the company was also a challenge from an organizational standpoint. Karim pondered the situation as his partners continued to discuss the items on the agenda that day. It was hard to imagine that all this had started eight years ago with a dream and the unstoppable passion of the stubborn teenager Karim had been.

Eight Years Back: The Seed of an Idea

In 2006, Karim Hossam was an average 16-year-old Egyptian. He was not much different from his friends except in one way: he was athletic and passionate about any sport that would induce an adrenaline rush. Karim was in Germany competing for Egypt in an international swimming competition when he walked into a sporting goods store. While he browsed inside the store he came across a snowboard; it was the first time it occurred to him that people actually snowboarded down snow-covered mountains and didn't just ski. International competitions require a lot of commitment, and Karim's swimming instructor kept his team to stringent rules such as sleeping early and constant practice, so the young man was not able to try out this new sport and soon found himself back in Egypt.

The Nile flows up the middle of Egypt, creating a valley of bountiful greenery that supported one of the Earth's oldest civilizations. To the east and west of that valley lies vast desert. There is almost no snow in Egypt, but there are plenty of sand dunes. The resourceful 16-year-old Karim decided to substitute rolling sand dunes for icy peaks and set about sketching the board he saw in Germany as well as he could remember it. He took his sketch to an ironsmith, who turned the sketch into a 20-kilogram reality. Karim got together some friends and excitedly went to try it out on a small sand dune on the outskirts of Cairo. It took the three young men an hour and a lot of energy to drag the heavy board up the small dune. They stepped back as Karim climbed onto the board. He leaned forward and prepared to rush down the dune. The board did not budge. An hour later, after his friends had tried giving him a push, angling the board differently, and tying it to a car and pulling it, the group came to the conclusion that the board was simply too heavy. The dejected Karim packed up his board and set off home.

Yet the idea was still too tempting for Karim to give up on that easily. While searching the Internet looking for a solution, he stumbled across the Dune Riders Federation in Oregon, in the United States. He contacted them and the federation sent him a design of the ideal board and advised him to use wood. He went to a carpenter with the design and then back to the same dune with the same group of friends, and this time his work was met with success.

In 2007, Karim, excited by his discovery and wanting to share it with other young people in Egypt, created an event on Facebook, open to everyone, to join him for a day of sandboarding on the outskirts of Cairo. This was a new concept, yet Karim felt that it would capture youth interest and that they would show up. He had five new boards made and brought a few burger patties and his father's barbecue grill, strapped them to the roof of his father's 4x4, and went to wait at the meeting point. Fifty people showed up. Karim, being optimistic, had expected five. Young Egyptians, tired of traditional excursions to the Pyramids or a museum, were looking for more adventurous ways to have fun. Soon Karim thought: why not turn this into a small business? He would use his dad's car, pack a few burgers and plenty of water, and turn this new idea into weekly excursions for which he would charge LE120, the equivalent of US$17; he even brought along a small boom box on which to play music and add to the fun.

Karim continued his venture for the next three years. He was not making much money but he was having fun and meeting new people, which was reason enough for him to keep doing it. By now the dune on the outskirts of Cairo that he had been frequenting was beginning to turn into a rough area. Karim's dad suggested he move operations to the Wahat Road, which was farther away from town and civilization, yet safer because no one was likely to come across the sandboarding party. Dune Raider had begun to take shape. The name, which Karim had used for his

Facebook page, was starting to become a brand. Meanwhile, the lack of market barriers was drawing a lot of competitors into the field.

Evolution of Dune Raider

In 2010, Karim was attempting to plan a local sandboarding competition. It was then that he happened to meet 21-year-old Mohamed Elwan, who was doing marketing consultations for Gold's Gym, an American fitness chain. As Mohamed learned more about sandboarding from Karim, he was overwhelmed with the possibilities for growth. They soon became partners; while Karim, who was passionate about the sport, stuck to organizing the actual excursions, Mohamed set about turning Dune Raider into a gold mine.

Mohamed decided very quickly that he would not engage with competitors in a race to the bottom. Let others drop prices to attract more customers; Dune Raider would offer a better service and charge for it. The first item to which Mohamed applied his differentiation strategy was the food. Out went the burgers and in came grilled chicken, with rice and salads. Next, he would provide unlimited snacks and soft drinks during the trip into the desert. Other competitors would charge extortionate prices for snacks or beverages, as sandboarders had no alternative in the desert but to pay. A better meal and not having to worry about snacks and beverages meant better service and warranted an increase in the ticket price from LE120 to LE160. Over the years Dune Raider kept improving the menu; it currently includes grilled chicken, kofta, rice, and two different salads.

Apart from improving the food, Elwan started marketing Dune Raider—and more specifically, the sandboarding competition. He decided to host a concert in the desert along with the competition and named the whole event "The Blues Revolution." He set up a stage in the desert and signed on two blues bands and a popular Egyptian band to play on the day of the competition. He then rented a Dodge Ram pickup truck and a band to play percussion and took them to Zamalek, an upscale neighbourhood which draws a trendy crowd, and held a flash concert that drew a crowd of around 400 people.

Five hundred tickets were sold for the concert/competition in the desert. All was going well and the upcoming competition was set to be a turning point for Dune Raiders to cementing their reputation for hosting the hippest events in the desert. But after everyone had arrived at the competition site, the Egyptian band called and canceled. According to the Funlozia team, the band members tired of the heat and, growing anxious from the long drive into the desert, decided to turn back. The crowd of 500 waiting to hear this exciting band, started growing restless and threatened to turn angry. Mohamed took to the stage and explained the situation to the upset fans. He then had one of the other bands start playing and started doing a comical dance on stage to encourage everyone to start dancing. Soon the misadventure was forgotten and everyone had a good time (See figures 5.1, 5.2, and 5.3).

Over time, the Dune Raider team began organizing more than sandboarding events. Their schedule included paintball and volleyball matches, as well as parasailing in the desert. As these new activities were added it became vital for Dune Raider to be able to guarantee customer safety. In January 2011, revolution broke out in Egypt and the winds of political change brought security risks as well. It was no longer safe to go wandering around in uninhabited areas as the image of the ever-powerful police force broke down. For a while, incidents of theft and kidnapping increased. However, over the years Dune Raiders had developed personal relationships with the Bedouin that inhabit the areas where they surfed the dunes. They started hiring the local Bedouin to police the area, and set up stringent rules that no camp should be set up within one kilometer of any other camp to guarantee the safety of customers. The team also had GPS systems installed in all of their buses in case they got lost or kidnapped in the desert, and bought a satellite phone to be used in case of emergency, as there is no mobile network signal in the desert. They started camping near ambulance points in case of accidents, and Karim signed up for comprehensive first-aid training courses. They made sure to check wind speed and the parachute before starting any parasailing activities and hired an ex-army officer trained as a paratrooper to be present.

The Creation of Funlozia

The year 2012 was a turning point for Dune Raider. In the first quarter Elwan was contacted by Aramex to organize a fun day of sandboarding in the desert for its employees. During the meeting Elwan was suddenly inspired to spin off the sandboarding event into a team-building event. He managed to convince the Aramex representative that he could provide a unique yet professional team-building event. Aramex was on board. All that remained was to figure out what a day of team-building might look like. For the next few days the Dune Raider team pored over management and human resource management books and planned team activities that would emphasize leadership skills. Apart from organizing the day in a professional way, they had to meet one challenge set by Aramex, which was to serve an ice cream cake in the desert at 5 p.m. at the end of the day. They managed to pull it off with the aid of a large cooler. As the feedback cards were collected they noticed that the two terms most used in describing them were "professional" and "innovative." Dune Raider was no longer just about sandboarding; a new line of business was born that would target corporate clients.

Up until this point, Dune Raider's operating season had been from September to May, as it was too hot to go into the desert during the summer. They organized their team-building days in Fayoum or other provinces with a cooler climate to offset the seasonality problem. Their team-building activities were always different and fresh. Once, they had teams find their way into the middle of Qarun Lake, a huge body of water in Fayoum, to obtain their team flag and find their way back to the shore. Another time, teams had to assemble go-karts, then communicate with the blindfolded driver of the kart to win the race. To be able to pull off this activity with confidence and safety, the Dune Raider team disassembled and reassembled the go-karts time and again to make sure nothing could go wrong that would compromise the safety of their customers. Their corporate clients include Commercial International Bank (CIB), one of the most prominent banks in Egypt, as well as multinationals such as Procter & Gamble and HSBC.

By now, Elwan had realized that the business's unique competency was in organizing fun, innovative events that were not necessarily limited to sandboarding. It seemed the right time to register as an official company, as all the events so far had taken place under the umbrella of the Dune Raider Facebook page. The company would be about organizing a fun experience. Funlozia was officially created in mid-2012, and registered as a company by Mohamed Elwan and Karim Hossam. The term itself was coined by Elwan, who had a habit of saying "that's so funlozia!" whenever he came across something unorthodox and entertaining. Funlozia had three lines of service that would each have its own brand. The first was the name-brand service that was the original source of fame for the company, Dune Raider, which organized one-day sandboarding excursions into the desert and included other fun activities such as paintballing and parasailing. The second service line, Go Camp, offered team-building events with flair for corporate clients in a professional yet adventurous manner. The third line, Camponita, organizes overnight adventure camping trips for individuals all over Egypt. Previously, the market had consisted solely of

Fig. 5.1. Media coverage of sandboarding in Egypt
Source: "It's Sand Boarding," *The Dome*, October 2010

Fig. 5.2. Media coverage of Dune Raider sandboarding
Source: *Sports and Fitness*, November 2009

LIFE STYLE

Selim

SANDBOARDING
COMING OF AGE IN EGYPT

Geographically located in the world's largest desert, Egypt has naturally been excluded from all kinds of winter sports. Egyptian daredevils have always looked at extreme sports such as, skiing and snow boarding in admiration and deep inside, a little envy for not being geographically compatible to slide down smooth slopes of crystal white snow. In the past few years however, things started looking up for adrenaline seekers in Egypt: Sand boarding, a sport rumored to have been invented by ancient Egyptians who surfed down golden dunes of sand on planks of hardened pottery and wood, has been reborn in the Sahara Desert.

By Yasmin Metwally

Contrary to what many believe, the sport has been around ever since its cousin sport, snowboarding, gained its popularity in the 1970's, but only took the spotlight within the past 10 years in different parts of the world. It has made its way back to what is said to be its country of birth, Egypt, where it is now not only considered one of the most exciting extreme outdoor activities, but also where the "Sand boarding World Championship" is specu- lated to be hosted for the first time in 2011.

The Sand boarding World Championships are held annually in Hirschau, Germany at Monte Kaolino, the site of Europe's largest sand hill. The idea of hosting such an important event in Egypt started with Kareem Hossam, a sand boarding enthusiast; whose passion for the sport began with his dream of sliding down steep sand slopes. He was determined to find the means to enable him to slide and tried

Fig. 5.3. Media coverage of Dune Raider sandboarding
Source: Yasmin Metwally, "Sandboarding: Coming of Age in Egypt," *Community Times*, June 2010

potential suppliers and providers; what had been missing was the event planner who creates and executes an integrated event. The founders saw Funlozia not only as a service provider but also as a consultant to meet customer requirements through integrated planning and execution of a whole event, be it a trip or a day of team building. They wanted Funlozia to be known for its innovative programs and high standards of quality.

The two partners made up the management team of Funlozia. Karim was operations manager and Elwan was general manager. Funlozia was growing exponentially and they had set a target to make twenty sales visits to sell their teambuilding services. Although the company had a small crew of full and part-timers, the brunt of the work fell on Elwan and Karim, as turnover was high and the staff simply did not have the required experience to carry through a deal. Enter Mohamed Fadly.

Early in 2013, Fadly, an engineering senior bursting with ideas, joined Funlozia as sales and marketing manager. He was offered a meager salary of LE1,200 per month—about US$171. He took the job anyway, simply because he had an idea for offering a wide array of water sport activities that he wanted to turn into a reality. The new partner set about creating a company portfolio and standardized proposals for sales visits. As a result of Fadly's sales efforts, Funlozia organized a sports day at the German University in Cairo, their first event outside the desert. This was enough motivation for Fadly to start recruiting a team of part-timers—students— in all major universities in Cairo. He also set up a good relationship with several student clubs at the American University in Cairo. The student organizations were clients of Funlozia and, at the same time, rich sources of a very valuable Funlozian asset: part-time employees who were fun loving and dynamic. College students who worked at Funlozia on a part-time basis made up the core of the crew after Fadly started handling sales in 2013. The university students fit seamlessly into the company envi- ronement. They helped the management team execute many tasks that needed the dynamism of young souls, which the managers failed to find in full-time graduates who were coming in mainly for an office job. Fun- lozia has an office, but most of the jobs are far from clerical. Before they began to hire sales and marketing part-timers at universities, Funlozia had had a full-time staff, but it quickly became clear that they were not doing much. According to Fadly, the responsibility of a Funlozia salesperson is to make new contacts and sales visits. Like at most other start-ups, a crew member should be flexible enough to take on other tasks outside their job description. The reality was that most full-timers who did not have a stake in the company spent most of their time in the office and were averse to taking part in operational activities because they were weary of roughing it in the desert.

The Market and the Competition

Funlozia is an entertainment solution provider serving several market segments with its three service brands, Dune Raider, Camponita, and Go Camp. Funlozia aspires to let its customers see Egypt through Funlozia's eyes, as Funlozia sees Egypt in a different way and has a unique perspective on how to enjoy Egypt's natural resources. Funlozia's offerings serve four main market segments: individuals, schools, universities, and corporations. In this big market, Funlozia competes with several companies that offer similar services, such as Remal, Campfire, Destination 31, and Kites. Indirectly, Funlozia also competes with all tour operators and similar service providers inside and outside Egypt who compete for the leisure time of clients. The following charts show Funlozia's market share in terms of the number of served customers in various market segments, as well as the overall sandboarding market share in comparison to the main direct competitors.

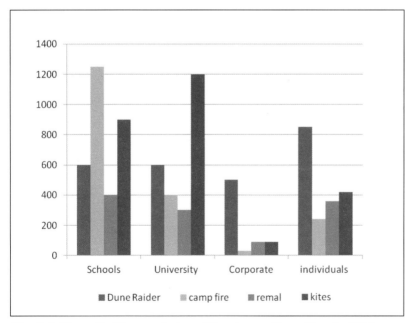

Fig. 5.4. Dune Raider market position in sandboarding in 2012 (number of customers) Source: *company records*

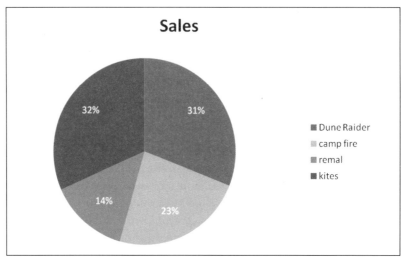

Fig. 5.5. Dune Raider overall market share in 2012
Source: *company records*

The Funlozian Culture

Perhaps the best word to describe the culture of this young company is simply 'Funlozia.' With a management trio in college and in their early twenties, the Funlozian culture is open, dynamic, fun, and unstoppable. Fadly says, "Of course there are people at the office, but most of us are out on the road, either making sales visits, organizing events, or out in the desert on camps and excursions." The Funlozia crew often works seven days a week. On weekdays they make sales visits to corporate leads, market Funlozia events, or coordinate and prepare for the trips. On weekends they are out in the desert, making sure their customers are having the time of their lives in the unique Funlozian experience. The Funlozia team adopted the slogan 'a new era of entertainment' and strives to bring out the daring part of each individual.

From Sales Manager to Partner

Fadly had only been working with the Funlozia crew for six months when he approached Karim Hossam and Mohamed Elwan to take him on as a partner in Dune Raider. In return for investing in a share of the capital, Fadly became a partner, holding an equal percentage of the equity in Funlozia and Dune Raider as Hossam and Elwan. In 2013, the burgeoning Funlozia was well on its way to growth, having served 4,000 customers, making over one million EGP in sales with a healthy profit margin. Despite its spectacular success, further growth might be difficult to come by given all the challenges Funlozia was facing. The time had come to organize house, open up new avenues for business, and find solutions to their challenges. The partners made their plans and staked the company's and their own futures in 2014.

Challenges and Strategies for Moving Forward

The biggest challenge to the Funlozia brand is the brand itself. While Funlozia has been the offical brand name of the event consultants, its Dune Raider arm is the one that has been known to the public ever since the launch of the Dune Raider Sandboarding Facebook page in 2008. The problem is that the Dune Raider brand limits the company in the eyes of the consumer to only sandboarding. The partners are concerned that by changing the name to Funlozia on their promotional material and online presence they would be sacrificing the brand equity of Dune Raider. At the same time, they find it necessary to differentiate the corporate team-building service and the overnight camping one as two distinct brands in their own right, as these services do not include sandboarding. The company's small size and organic growth strategy make it all the more challenging to build three different brands and make them stand out in the market. A huge amount of funds will be needed for brand building.

Another challenge Funlozia is facing is related to the competition- not in itself, but in what it does to the market. The political and economic instability that Egypt has lived through in the past three years has made consumers extremely price-sensitive. Given the low entry barriers, it was not difficult for copycats looking to make an easy profit to hire a bus and launch a sandboarding event on Facebook. It became harder to sell Dune Raider's LE250 trips when the competitors' offer was priced as low as LE120, albeit at a lower standard. According to Fadly, the real problem lies in the fact that individuals have a rough time on a lower-quality trip and therefore are not willing to try any more sandboarding trips. The customer does not realize that the poor service could have been avoided had he or she gone on the trip with Dune Raiders, and the customer is lost to the industry at large. Also, the negative word of mouth discourages potential customers from trying out sandboarding. As if that was not bad enough, the Funlozia crew have trouble educating consumers about safety and differentiating themselves from competitors, because any written document would get stolen and posted on their competitors' Facebook page verbatim. Event photos and the brand name, Dune Raider, would also get stolen by competitors trying to distort the image of their service. Me-too competitor tactics, outright theft of Dune Raider material published on social media, and low-priced, poor-service offerings are wreaking havoc with the company's trendy and fun image and the market it created, trip by trip and customer by hard-won customer.

A third challenge for Funlozia relates to their service strategy and the service mix they are offering their clients under their three brands—Dune Raider, Go Camp, and Camponita. The management team is currently negotiating an important strategic tension that is quite common for young companies about to embark on a growth trajectory. The partners cannot seem to keep up with the ever-widening variety of events and services they are offering their clients; new services are being created at a very fast pace. This expansion is crucial to support the growth in Funlozia's sales revenues, especially during the current period of political unrest and economic downturn in Egypt. At the same time, Funlozia risks diluting its brand identity and losing strategic focus if it is lured into excessive expansion. Focus is also important to direct the limited resources of a young company effectively and to build the core competencies and regulate organizational processes in specific lines of work.

Funlozia is, however, opening up new horizons in all its service lines. Dune Raider is preparing to host the 2015 International Sandboarding Championship and positioning itself as a professional sandboarding hub, with professional sandboarding instructors. The Go Camp strategy has favored setting up long-term relationships with a few customers, namely multinational companies, travel agencies, and top university student organizations. It aims to be the event consultant for these entities. The sales team has managed to set up such a relationship with Aramex, Tez Travel Agency, and several clubs at AUC. Instead of marketing online and trying to reach a mass market, Go Camp now seeks to have brand ambassadors and sales representatives who are students at various universities in Egypt, and who are better able to get the word out on upcoming events, trips, and the Funlozia brand in general. By targeting those customers who have the ability and willingness to pay Funlozia's higher trip prices, the company can focus on maintaining its higher quality and coming up with fresh ideas.

Funlozia has also added new excursions, which will open new avenues of growth. In a little over a year Fadly managed to turn his idea of an adventure beach into a reality at the Emirates Heights resort on the Egyptian north coast. The company has also set up a line of purely cultural and educational trips to areas that receive little interest despite their cultural significance, such as a valley containing the prehistoric remains of whales, the oldest Roman remains in Egypt, and the islands of Nubia. To dovetail with this, Funlozia has also snagged the large account, previously handled by Thomas Cook in Egypt, of Educational Trips, which organizes trips in Egypt for children between the ages of eight and eighteen, from all over the world. Last but not least, the company is working on obtaining a license from the Egyptian Ministry of Tourism to allow it to advertise their trips internationally and set up bookings and accommodations for tourists to visit Egypt. In short, they can function as a fully-fledged travel agency. With so much going on at Funlozia, maintaining a sound strategy is key.

A fourth challenge for Funlozia relates to managerial and human resource aspects. With a plethora of service introductions and activities at Funlozia, the three partners have been spreading themselves quite thin trying to cope with all that is happening at the company. A managerial and organizational infrastructure that will keep up with Funlozia's rapid growth has yet to be put in place. Fadly, Elwan, and Karim need to keep track of most of the work details themselves, which has become overwhelming. Earlier, when they had several full-time employees in marketing and operations, they used delegation to alleviate part of the workload. High employee turnover posed a serious obstacle. Several employees who had received training at the company in operations, sales, or marketing departed with the know-how and Funlozia's contact databases to set up as competitors. Feeling that they were wasting their valuable time training would-be competitors, the partners decided to take matters back into their own hands. Hiring part-time university students who do very well as brand ambassadors solved the full-time employee turnover problem. College students bring their own kind of trouble, however. While eager to work, students do not have the experience to make sales visits to multinational corporations.

The Funlozia culture is a very open and inclusive culture that treats every member of the company as an insider, whether they are full- or part-time employees. Strategic and financial issues and even numbers are shared openly in the office. Fadly was shocked once to find that some financial information that was discussed in the presence of one of the part-time student employees was widely known in the office by other members who had nothing to do with the issue. Training these part-timers takes a long time, so in the meantime most of the work falls to the three partners, who have lost customers and missed important meetings because they are not able to cope. In addition, operating procedures have not been standard-ized, so sometimes on the eve of an event there are still loose threads as well as some customers who have not paid for their tickets. The situation remains unsettled and Funlozia urgently needs to come up with a solution to enable them to delegate work and standardize operating procedures.

6 Evaluation of Pan-Islamic Investment Banking in the Middle East: The Case of ICD

Ali Soliman

Introduction

The Islamic Corporation for the Development of the Private Sector (ICD), a subsidiary of Islamic Development Bank Group, was founded in 1999 and is based in Jeddah, Saudi Arabia. ICD aims to develop its member countries through investment in the private sector. It offers long- and short-term financing, and advisory and arrangement services. It is required to offer only sharia-compliant finance such as *musharaka* (where capital is provided by two or more parties), diminishing *musharaka*, *mudharba* (where all investment comes from one investor, and the remaining work is the complete responsibility of the entrepreneur, or company itself), leasing, installment sale, manufacturing contract finance, *murabaha*, and *bai salam* (where payment is made for goods to be delivered at a future date), to medium-sized businesses in the Organization of Islamic Cooperation (OIC) countries.

Overview of Islamic Banking and Finance

During the last four decades, Islamic banking and finance has witnessed phenomenal growth worldwide. Globally, the annual growth rate exceeds 15 percent per year. In some countries in the Middle East and Asia, it is accepted as the foremost alternative banking option for millions of customers. Such rapid growth brought with it many challenges as well as subsequent innovations.

History and Development of ICD

ICD was incorporated in November 1999 (AH 1420) and started operating the following year. What makes ICD unique is that it is the first attempt to create a multilateral financial institution that operates in the OIC's 57 countries, and offers Islamic finance without requiring sovereign guarantees for its lending. Its parent company, the Islamic Development Bank (IsDB or the 'Bank')[1] has been around longer and has been the subject of academic research (Kuhn, 1982).

The objectives and mandate of ICD were greatly affected by those of its parent company, IsDB. One of these objectives was to foster solidarity among OIC countries.[2] The Bank was also mandated to help development in member countries and had offered, until then, investment funds to governments and public entities.

The call to establish a specialized corporation to finance the private sector started in the early 1990s after the fall of the Soviet Union and the accession of new members from Central Asia. To ascertain the need for such a specialized corporation, an international committee was established, a special study commissioned, and many discussions by the board of directors of IsDB ensued.

Finally, in November 1999, the Articles of Agreement of ICD were adopted, creating an international specialized institution to "promote, in accordance with the principles of the Shari'a, the economic development of its member countries by encouraging the establishment, expansion, and modernization of private enterprises."

The original authorized capital stock of ICD was US$1.0 billion, with US$500 million having initially been opened for subscription. Fifty percent of this amount was allocated to IsDB and was fully paid in three installments. Further, under the Articles, some US$150 million of ICD capital was allocated to IsDB member countries, representing 30 percent of ICD's capital initially available for subscription, with the balance thereof being available for subscription by public institutions of member countries. In 2010, the board of directors recommended an increase of subscribed capital to US$1.0 billion.

The distribution of capital shares of member countries in ICD was similar to that of IsDB. This again ensured that almost 85 percent of the shares are in the hands of oil-exporting countries, Turkey,[3] and Egypt. As countries with financial surpluses are likely to be better off than the other member countries, this stipulation would strengthen the solidarity aspect of this corporation. The second feature was that ICD would only finance private sector projects in member countries. This new objective was in recognition of the trend, following the collapse of the Soviet Union and the ascendency of free-market orientation worldwide, to transfer "the financing of development projects from the public to private sector."[4] A third, novel objective of ICD was for it to use exclusively sharia-compliant modes of financing in the private sector. This novel objective has a certain 'missionary' element in which ICD is used not only as a vehicle to inculcate private sector development ideals, but also to propagate Islamic finance modes in member countries.[5]

Role and Performance of ICD

Islamic financial institutions are expected to pursue a number of 'ethical' objectives in addition to making profits and seeking sustainability and growth. ICD's objectives, listed prominently in the Articles of Agreement, included, among other things, 1) to help in the development of member countries, 2) to strengthen their comparative advantage, c) to help create jobs, and d) to generate foreign currency receipts. In addition ICD was expected to follow normal business and commercial objectives, namely, to be self-reliant and to generate reasonable profits.

It is a well-known managerial dictum that as an organization's objectives multiply, the task of executive management becomes more complicated. To help control the number of evaluation parameters here we evaluate the performance of ICD in three main areas: its developmental impact on member countries, responsibility toward staff and clients, and overall financial performance.

Impact on Member Countries

Spread and size of operations

ICD has fulfilled its mandate by providing finance and assistance to private-sector projects in countries with a special need for longer-term foreign currency investment funds. Figure 6.1 gives the growth of the value of approvals and disbursements for the years AH 1421–32 (2000–11). A more detailed country distribution of project approval is shown in table 6.1.

At the end of AH 1432 (2011), ICD's accumulated approvals since it began operations reached US$2.17 billion distributed among 218 projects in 35 countries. The cumulative gross approvals, according to mode of finance, included US$766.07 million of equity, US$535.77 million of *murabaha*,[6] US$526.53 million of *ijara* (leasing), US$223.13 million of installment sales,[7] and US$119.14 million of *istisna'a* (where the seller

Fig. 6.1. ICD project approvals and disbursements (US$ million)

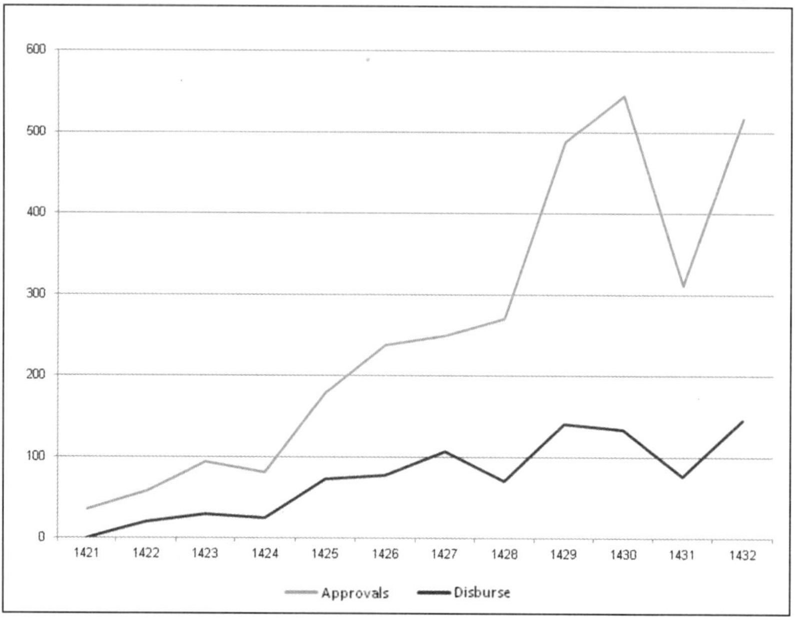

Source: Author, compiled from ICD Annual Reports, various issues.

is expected to manufacture the goods he wished to sell).[8] This distribution results in more than 35 percent of total commitments in the form of equity, and 24.3 percent in the form of leasing. This readiness to participate in the capital of development projects in member countries in the form of equity affirms the Islamic nature of ICD's finance, as it is willing to share the risk with its clients (Pappas and Izzeldin 2011).

Another feature of ICD's operations is the way in which it apportions its funds among countries. A priori, the mandate of ICD would lead us to expect lower-income countries to receive a high percentage of financing. Analysis of the portfolio (see table 6.1) affirms this orientation. We have grouped ICD beneficiaries into four income groups: countries with per capita income (PCI) of less than US$2,000; US$2,001–5,999; US$6,000–20,000, and above US$20,000. The results (shown in table 6.2) indicate that ICD tried to spread its financing among all income groups. Also, ICD was sensitive to the needs of some of its least-developed countries (Pakistan, Sudan, and Yemen) and those with an acute shortage of medium- and long-term foreign currency funds (Azerbaijan and Syria, during the study period): they received a high share of total ICD financing.

Table 6.1. Distribution of ICD's cumulative operations by country, US$ million

Country	2002	2008	2011
1.1 Qatar	5.0	16.2	16.2
1.2 Bahrain		23.0	50.7
1.3 Kuwait		11.1	14.1
1.4 Saudi Arabia	8.0	275.4	411.0
1.5 UAE	2.0	40.9	50.9
2.1 Algeria		0.0	23.0
2.2 Azerbaijan		55.2	113.8
2.3 Iran	6.0	59.9	114.9
2.4 Kazakhstan		15.5	15.5
2.5 Lebanon		7.0	7.0
2.6 Libya		30.0	73.0
2.7 Malaysia		12.5	24.5
2.8 Maldives		4.0	31.7
3.1 Egypt	5.0	33.9	67.4
3.2 Gabon		14.2	14.2
3.3 Indonesia		13.8	68.8
3.4 Jordan		44.8	47.1
3.5 Uzbekistan		7.2	92.2
3.6 Kyrgyzstan		18.4	18.4
3.7 Pakistan		62.2	107.2
3.8 Senegal		6.6	15.5
3.9 Syria	10.0	62.6	151.0
3.10 Tajikistan		2.5	12.5
3.11 Turkmenistan		0.0	5.0
4.1 Bangladesh		5.3	60.3
4.2 Burkina Faso		3.5	3.5
4.3 Djibouti		4.0	4.0
4.4 Gambia		14.2	21.3
4.5 Guinea		1.3	2.8
4.6 Mali		0.0	21.3
4.7 Mauritania		53.5	59.8
4.8 Niger		0.9	11.2
4.9 Sudan		46.1	49.0
4.10 Yemen	7.0	134.7	162.9
4.11 Uganda		0.0	10.0
5.0 Regional	13.0	79.4	218.8
TOTAL	63.6	1159.8	2170.5

First digit of the number shows income group: high (1), high middle (2), low middle (3), and low (4). "Regional" denotes projects that would benefit more than one country.

Source: Author, compiled from ICD Annual Reports, various issues.

Table 6.2. Distribution of ICD financial commitments by income groups

Income group	Income range	Amount received (million)	% share
High income	>$20,000	$542.9	25.0
High middle income	$6,000–19,999	$403.4	18.5
Lower middle income	$2,000–5,999	$599.3	27.6
Lower income	<$2,000	$406.1	18.7
Regional projects	———	$218.8	10.0

Source: ICD Annual Report, various issues; World Bank 2012

Intervention in Sudan

Sudan is a good example of ICD's intervention in a least-developed country. Total ICD financing for Sudan, up to 2011, stood at US$49.0 million, or 2.25 percent of total approvals. ICD promoted an international Islamic bank (Bank Byblos Africa), financed a major telephone and mobile operator (Sudatel),[9] extended finance to a project to improve silo facilities in Port Sudan, and another to increase the efficiency of oil fields. ICD also participated in a cement project in Berber, and tried to help a renovation of the aircraft of a small local airline. All of these projects addressed serious needs of the country. Four of these projects came to fruition with no difficulty while one (the silos) was greatly delayed due to managerial problems and associated cost overrun. The airline project never materialized due to the withdrawal of a major investor.

In all of these projects a strong association with foreign capital or entrepreneurs was established. This association was designed either to reduce ICD's exposure or to ensure success of the project by collaborating with a foreign technical partner. Parent companies of Lebanese, Emirati, and Yemeni origin took the lead. This fulfilled another ICD mandate, to help foreign direct investment flows, especially among its member countries.

Intervention in Yemen

In 2011, total approvals for Yemen stood at US$162.90 million, or 7.5 percent of total approvals. ICD's intervention in Yemen followed similar lines to Sudan's, with support to a major healthcare facility, a mobile company, an Islamic bank, a cement project, and other industrial projects. Also, ICD invested in a domestic airline. Again, Saudi and expatriate Yemeni investors were instrumental in some of these projects. As there were expectations of high profits, the ICD board of directors took an additional risk and approved to syndicate a large portion of the company's shares. In the end, in 2011, ICD held 45 percent of company shares and was exposed to major impairment due to the political turmoil during the 'Arab Spring.'

Intervention in Azerbaijan and Syria

The intervention of ICD in Azerbaijan and Syria provides two models of how middle-income countries were approached. Both countries had a severe shortage of foreign currency and high margins for long-term financing.

Syria had longer traditions in private-sector development and a viable industrial sector. ICD directly financed projects in that country, especially in industry, mostly in the form of leasing, installment sale, and *murabaha*. No equity participation was taken, as most of the projects were family-owned. It also offered short-term finance to companies with good export prospects. Before the civil troubles of 2011, many projects of the first phase were successfully completed and ICD financing repaid. One project folded due to the death of the promoter and ICD had to take possession of the project to protect its interests. In fact, the ICD experience confirmed that the ability to take over and run a project is the ultimate guarantee for industrial lending. In 2011, total approvals for Syria stood at US$151.00 million, or 7 percent of total approvals.

In Azerbaijan, most financing was through lines of finance to local banks. In a later stage ICD dominated investment funds and leasing companies were created. The impact of such a policy is likely increased cost and risk profile of administering the funds, as will be seen below. In 2011, total approvals for Azerbaijan stood at US$113.80 million, or 5.25 percent of total approvals.

Role of ICD in spreading Islamic banking and finance in OIC countries

ICD benefited from its association with the Islamic Development Bank group. More and more countries were opening the door for Islamic finance. In the first few years of operations, ICD concentrated on the core countries of the Middle East. These countries were more exposed to the precepts of Islamic finance, and were easier to access geographically and culturally. Later ICD spread its operations to African and Asian countries. In the Commonwealth of Independent States (CIS) countries, the real push started after the organization of the annual meetings of the IsDB Group in Almaty, Kazakhstan in 2003. These countries sought to receive lines of finance from ICD which would make small and medium loans available to local entities on sharia-compatible terms. ICD found this modality a fast way of introducing Islamic finance to local industry through conventional banks.[10] Later, ICD helped establish a number of new Islamic banks.[11] The demand for Islamic modes of finance was driven not only by 'ideological' motives, but also by the desire to compensate for the paucity of credit available for private projects and especially for SMEs in these countries.[12] The scarcity of credit to the private sector was reflected in large interest margins in many CIS countries already enjoying an economic boom (engendered by high oil prices, foreign aid, and the Afghan war next door).[13] Due to its development role, ICD's finance facilities were offered at variable rates of 7 to 9 percent (most of these were on leasing, *murabaha*, and *bai ajil*[14] finance modes). ICD also took some equity positions in local banks and enterprises.

Role of ICD in promoting local entrepreneurship and economic development

In any project appraisal it is important to give sufficient weight to the credibility and experience of the project's entrepreneur. ICD's management added another requirement. In Middle East and Muslim cultures, trust is a basic element in business dealings. ICD management realized that close relations of trust and collaboration guaranteed the realization of a project's objectives, and in many cases it assured the repayment of loan financing. In some cases the relationship exceeded that between a financier and borrower, as ICD acted as if it were the owner and offered operational advice and management support. In other words, ICD acted as an equity fund even when no direct equity investment was involved. Such a close relationship has its own risks, however. This is confirmed by the findings of theoretical research regarding the risk profile of Islamic and smaller banks.[15]

The record shows that ICD had a role in helping local entrepreneurs expand their operations. In the UAE, ICD helped a medical college acquire and equip a teaching hospital, and a Saudi health group used a syndicated financing of US$100 million to expand into Yemen. In both Kazakhstan and the UAE, ICD supported the attempt of local entrepreneurs to compete against some of the big names in oil services. In other cases ICD helped enhance the local comparative advantage, for example, by supporting the textile industry in Syria and in Uzbekistan, and supporting sprouting IT technology companies in Egypt, Jordan, and the UAE. ICD helped finance new telephone companies in Sudan, Syria, and Yemen.

ICD's Responsibility to Staff and Clients

It is essential for an 'ethical' institution to do well for its employees (Zubairu, Sakariyau, and Dauda 2012; IsDB 2005). One of the biggest challenges facing ICD management in the early years was expanding its staff and cultivating team spirit and the sense of impartiality and loyalty commensurate with an international organization. These factors brought staff affairs to the forefront. Many staff candidates were eager to work in a pan-Islamic organization and to serve the *umma* (the Islamic nation). Many thought that Jeddah was an attractive place to live, as it is a modern city with many shopping venues, accessible airline routes, and proximity to the Muslim holy sites. Some of the international staff thought that life in Jeddah was especially difficult, however, as cultural and social amenities were limited. Also, the opportunity for their wives to find jobs was restricted. This added to their feeling of alienation. Many reverted back to their national groups and resisted assimilation. So an additional management challenge was to enhance team spirit and help newcomers overcome the feeling of isolation, and to ensure bonding among staff. The CEO sponsored a number of social activities and professional sessions. These included organized sports events, fully subsidized sport facility memberships for staff and spouses, family gatherings, and Ramadan iftar parties. Professionally, the staff met monthly to discuss operational matters over breakfast, and went on several retreats away from headquarters to discuss strategic issues. In addition the executive management followed a five-pronged approach to staff affairs:

1. Increase the number and diversity of the staff. As the bank dealt with more countries, it needed to learn more about the business and socio-economic environment in these new areas. A diversified staff would facilitate the acquisition of this information.

2. Improve capacity and knowledge of the staff through training, and attendance at conferences and seminars.

3. Improve staff relations, loyalty, and cohesion through joint meetings and activities. A bimonthly bulletin was also issued and an open management policy was adopted. Staff members were encouraged in open meetings to discuss their operational views and suggest policy changes.

4. Institute a transparent and equitable control and accountability system. An incentive bonus system was adopted from the second year of operations. By the fourth, the 'Bonus Fund' rose to about 3 percent of annual profits. This pioneering ICD initiative was adopted later by the parent company.

5. Put staff and family welfare at the forefront. A flex-time work schedule was instituted from the first year to accommodate the different working habits and domestic responsibilities of the international staff. In addition, ICD followed the human resources rules of its parent company, IsDB. These included generous expatriate benefits such as travel for the families, home leave, and health and education benefits.

Financial Performance of ICD

Growth of assets and equity

ICD was able to grow steadily in terms of assets and shareholders' equity (see table 6.3). On average, total assets grew at 22.26 percent per year from US$91.2 million to US$844.75 million from 2000 to 2011 (AH 1421–1432), and equity grew by 20.25 percent per year. Asset growth was a reflection shareholders' generosity who raised their capital participation, and, in addition, IsDB extended US$100 million in subordinated loans. Later increases in profits helped improve equity and total assets.

Table 6.3. Growth of ICD's assets and equity, millions of US$

Year	Total Assets	Equity
2000 (1421)	91.2	90.7
2001 (1422)	194.3	186.3
2002 (1423)	277.4	274.5
2003 (1424)	284.9	281.8
2004 (1425)	314.3	311.8
2005 (1426)	320.3	311.6
2006 (1427)	367.6	352.5
2007 (1428)	420.5	399.3
2008 (1429)	472.8	457.5
2009 (1430)	655.0	514.4
2010 (1431)	717.1	572.6
2011 (1432)	844.8	689.3

Hegira Years (AH) in parentheses
Source: ICD Annual Report, various issues.

Revenues and expenses

Profitability is a good indicator of the efficiency and stability of a financial institution. This statement remains true even if ICD was requested to pursue other goals. In this respect, ICD was profitable for most years of its operation. We can divide the first twelve years of ICD's existence into three distinct periods. The first was a formative period extending through the first four years. In those years total expenses were growing faster than accrued revenues. During the first four years, expenses were growing at 86.42 percent per year while revenues were growing at 46.88 percent. The faster rate of growth of expenses was justified by the need to build corporate capacity through staff hiring, furnishing offices, preliminary marketing trips, and engaging of consultants or local representatives.

In the next four years, AH 1425–28 (2004–2007), the fruits of the earlier labors began to be harvested. Expenses were growing at 25.2 percent per year while revenues were growing at 38.3 percent. During those years, two things can be noticed. First, the corporation was able diversify its income, not only from margins of investment operations, but also from capital gains and consultancy and advisory services. In addition, the executive management realized that in a period of highly volatile foreign exchange, ICD needed to try to preserve the value of its holdings of liquid funds. After getting requisite approvals from the board of directors, up to 30 percent of liquid funds were kept in international currencies other than the US dollar. Modest profits were realized from these activities. Another effort to have a diversified equity portfolio in developed capital markets in its member countries was not as successful. Investments in a holding company in Iran sustained large losses due to the deterioration of the political situation and the collapse of the Tehran stock market around 2005. A small investment in a diversified, locally managed portfolio (2003–2006) in Malaysia barely broke even. Much better success was realized in equity holding of subsidiary companies. Handsome capital gains were realized in the equity of companies in Egypt (Raya Holding), Yemen (Saba'fon), and Bahrain (Injazat Technology Fund).

In the final four years of this study, AH 1429–32 (2008–11), expenses were growing at 29.2 percent per year while revenues were declining by 2.4 percent. Figure 6.2 portrays a major shift in the revenues and expenses profile.

These dramatic changes in both revenues and expenses suggest a radical departure in policies and/or market conditions. The years 2008–11 were years of recovery from the drastic ramifications of the financial crisis. The executive management tried to keep a steady course and claimed that they, along with many other Islamic banks, were not much affected by the crisis.[16] It is unlikely, however, that ICD escaped unscathed. We are thus impelled to look for other reasons for the deterioration of profitability at ICD in the last four years under study.

Figure 6.2. ICD's revenues and expenses, AH 1421–32, US$ millions

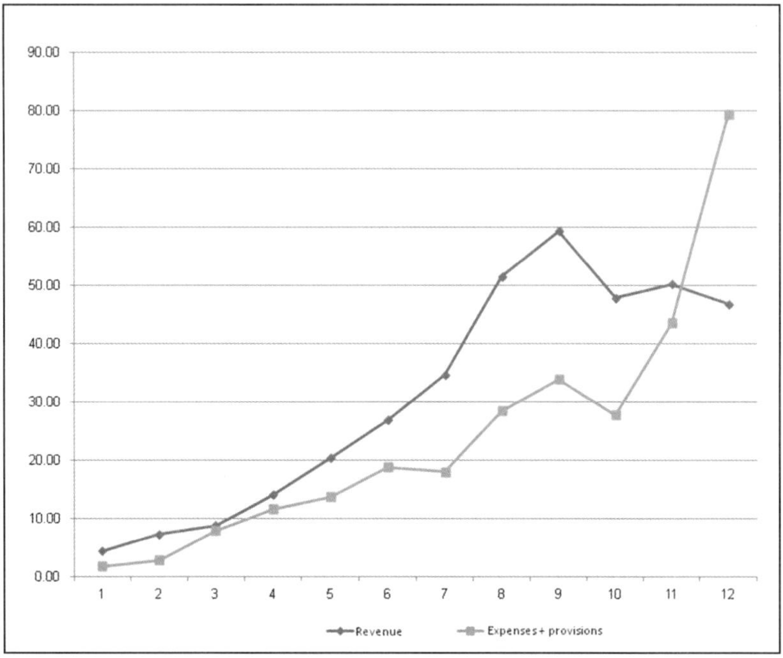

Source: Author, compiled from ICD Annual Reports, various issues

On the one hand, expenses (especially for staff and administration) exploded. On the other hand, revenues decelerated and actually went down in the last three years. The inevitable result was the realization of substantial losses for the first time in the life of the corporation in AH 1432 (2011).

The deceleration of profits could be the natural result of three intrinsic tendencies:

i) The very rapid expansion in operations in new countries, especially in Africa and in the Far East, pursued by the corporation in the last years under study. As table 6.1 shows, the number of countries and projects increased exponentially from only seven, with total approvals of US$63.0 million, at the end of the second year of operations, AH 1422, to thirty-two countries with a total approvals value of US$1.159 billion six years later, in AH 1429, an eighteen-fold increase. Again, four years later, in AH 1432 (2011), the value of total approvals almost doubled to US$2.17 billion in thirty-five countries plus regional operations. This policy, possibly adopted to respond to claims by poorer members that they were not getting a fair share, was contrary to a policy that would build on successes achieved in some markets without trying to cover all members. A more concentrated presence would have ensured more rational utilization of ICD's limited internal resources. Also, economies of scale would have been assured as more than one project is approached during the same trip. This was the practice in the frugal early years of operations. To open any new market, one or two general marketing presentations would be organized with the collaboration of the local chamber of commerce and industry, or the equivalent. On the periphery, individual projects would be entertained. During follow-up, visits to existing projects can be undertaken. Meantime, concurrent visits to local officials would ensure government support. This 'bunching' was meant to ensure efficient utilization of resources. Needless to say, shareholders, in effect government officials, especially in African countries, were not quite happy to wait until the ICD bus would reach their stop. They wanted one ICD project or more here and now. As a result, sprinkling ICD projects to cover more countries pleased the constituency but raised operational expenses.

Thus, we can conclude that the widespread distribution of ICD presence in member countries, although 'egalitarian' from the beneficiaries' point of view, may have in fact engendered diseconomies of scale and increased business risk. ICD, which had to operate from one principal office in Jeddah, was getting more and more distant from its familiar ground and expertise. Management and transportation costs also increased in proportion to the geographical distance.

On the other hand, ICD started a number of regional funds for CIS, African, and East Asian countries. These regional funds were justified by the need to be closer to the market and hopefully would lead to lower operating costs.

ii) The second reason for increased losses in the later years of ICD's life seems to be due to its increased appetite for additional risk exposure. In the first eight years of the corporation, ICD assiduously followed its own 'General Investment Guidelines'[17] and its equity participation did not exceed 33 percent of capital in any project. By contrast, the annual report for AH 1432 (2011) lists eleven equity contributions where ICD's share exceeds 40 percent. In four of these projects ICD held 100 percent of capital. This is definitely not in line with prudent policy or established investment guidelines. In addition, such a policy seems to contravene an additional stipulation in the Articles of Agreement that ICD should not be directly involved in the management of its subsidiary companies. The rationale for this stipulation made practical sense. ICD did not have enough local presence or intelligence to be able to run a local company. Also, ICD may not have the technical know-how of the particular industry. Thus, it should not have created or managed wholly-owned subsidiaries.

The executive management had its reasons for desiring to promote and initially fully-owned subsidiaries in member countries, and later divest them to the public or specialized technical partners. The cases under review do not seem to fill these presumed criteria, however. Three of the fully-owned subsidiaries are leasing companies in Azerbaijan, Saudi Arabia, and Uzbekistan. Why ICD would engage in these activities is not clear. Leasing companies have a continuous need for additional financing and are normally associated with local banks.

The last case, investments in Syria, could represent a matter of force majeure and not policy. ICD had to take over the assets of a defunct company upon the death of a delinquent debtor. Thus a wholly-owned holding company was created to manage such assets and similar new ventures.

iii) The third reason for the increased losses seems to have been accelerating administrative expenses. Total ICD staff almost doubled in the last four years. New and expensive additional offices in downtown Jeddah were rented. The remuneration of ICD staff was greatly increased, including expensive retirement packages for the higher echelons. It seemed that the idealistic first years where service to the *umma* was the guiding principle are over. ICD is now more of a 'normal' investment company than before.

Conclusion

IsDB took it upon itself to create a new entity that competes with local private-sector banks. One unique feature of ICD was that it was fully conceived, promoted, and managed by Less Developed Countries' (LDC) professionals. What distinguishes IsDB from the World Bank may be the fact that ICD had a different board of directors. Also, a strong element of public interest and a desire to serve the *umma* was intrinsic to this success. This might be why the International Finance Corporation (IFC), which is supported by the World Bank, took two years to approve its first loan and six years to engage in the first equity, whereas ICD had its first equity participation in the first year, and had six operations by year two.

In both ICD and IFC, equity participation was the main source of revenue. The meager margins realized on loan or finance operations, respectively, could not cover overhead expenses. In the Middle East, due to the vagaries of political upheavals and international interventions, equity participation added further vulnerabilities. Economic sanctions on Iran and Arab Spring dislocations, especially in Libya, Syria, and Yemen, caused substantial losses. ICD's main success was in the forging of a multinational team that is able to work effectively and efficiently. This type of civil esprit de corps is not easy to develop, and is a real hidden asset of the organization.

The experience of ICD confirmed the importance of follow-up of project finance. Equity participation and board membership in affiliated companies ensures such follow-up and reduces moral hazard. Also, it seems that ICD was more ethical than other multilateral institutions, as it has tried to practice cross-subsidization by offering lower-than-market margins in more needy markets, and takes a higher risk through *musharaka* than traditional banks.

Notes

1   IsDB was created in 1975 as a solidarity and development bank for members of the OIC. It was modeled after an earlier example of Islamic banks started at a modest scale in the town of Mit Ghamr in Egypt; see Ismail 2011.

2   Kuhn demonstrates that in the few years following the oil boom of the mid-seventies, the international aid of Arab oil exporters far exceeded the target set by the UN, which was 0.7 percent of GDP. The United Arab Emirates contributed a stupendous 16 percent of its GDP while Saudi Arabia shelled out 3.15 percent (Kuhn 1982, 58).

3   Turkey, a signatory to the ICD Articles of Agreement, has failed to ratify it, as the opposition party in parliament objected to the phrase "in accordance with Shari'a" in the Preamble. They considered such terms to be contrary to the secular nature of the state. This particular difficulty did not prevent Turkey from engaging in Islamic finance operations, even with ICD.

4   Preamble of the Articles of Agreement.

5   The use of word 'Shari' or 'Sharia' (in Article 3) was not well understood by the political elites in member or non-member countries. The author believes that this misunderstanding was behind the delay of ratification of the Articles of Agreement in at least four countries, namely Morocco, Nigeria, Oman, and Turkey. (For countries that have not ratified the agreement, see ICD's Annual Report for AH 1429 (2008)).

6   *Murabaha* is a cost-plus contract in which the bank agrees to buy goods on behalf of the borrower. The borrower gets delivery of the goods and pays later (normally within two years) at a higher price.

7   Installment sales are similar to *mudaraba* except that the repayment period is longer.

8   This is a contract where a contractor promises to build and deliver a product to the client. In this case the bank will play the role of financier and contractor. It is the least-used form of present-day Islamic finance.

9   The Sudatel project was a syndicated loan under the leadership of a Bahraini offshore bank.
10   One such line of finance was to the International Bank of Azerbaijan (IBA), the largest bank in that country, along with two smaller banks. The same experience was repeated in Tajikistan.
11   In Kyrgyzstan in 2007, ISDB offered technical assistance to the government to help change banking laws to allow for Islamic modes of finance.
12   The World Bank Ease of Doing Business (2010) lists many of ICD's member countries among the most difficult in terms of availability of credit. The list included Sudan, Syria, Uzbekistan, and Yemen.
13   The cost of medium-term loans in US dollar funds averaged between 16 and 22 percent at the time (2002–2004).
14   Literally, *bai ajil* means 'postponed sale,' or sale for a deferred payment.
15   Contrary to the conventional wisdom, which asserts that lenders enjoy a lower risk than shareholders as they have first claim on assets and guarantees, Pappas and Izzeldin (2011) found Islamic banks to have a lower risk profile. These findings were confirmed in ICD's experience.
16   See "Letter from CEO," ICD Annual Report for AH 1431 (2010).
17   These 'Guidelines' were prepared by an international consultant entrusted with preparing the business plan, and approved by the board of directors before start-up of operations in 2000.

References

Akhtar, M. Farhan, K. Ali, and S. Sadaqat. 2011. "Liquidity Risk Management: A Comparative Study between Conventional and Islamic Banks of Pakistan." *Interdisciplinary Journal of Research in Business* 1, no. 1: 35–44.
Grais, W. 2008. "Sharia' Compliance and Governance of Sharia' Compliant Financial Intermediation." Unpublished.
Haniffa, Roszaini, and Mohammad Hudaib. 2007. "Exploring the Ethical Identity of Islamic Banks via Communication in Annual Reports." *Journal of Business Ethics* 76, no. 1: 97–116.
Harris, M., and A. Raviv. 1978a. "Optimal Incentive Contracts with Imperfect Information." Mimeograph, revised. Carnegie Mellon University.
———. 1978b. "Some Results on Incentive Contracts." *American Economic Review* 68, no. 1: 20–30.
ICD (Islamic Corporation for the Development of the Private Sector). 1999. "General Investment Guidelines." Jeddah.
———. 2000–12. *Annual Reports.* Jeddah.
———. 2005–2007. *Bulletin.* various issues. http://www.icd-IsDB.org
International Finance Corporation. "IFC History." http://ifcext.ifc.org/ifcext/masterinternet.nsf/AttachmentsByTitle/ifctFS.htm/$FILE/ifctFS.htm
International Financial Consultants. 2007. "Evaluation of ICD's Performance and Suggested Restructuring Plan (EPRP)." July. Toronto. Unpublished.
IsDB (Islamic Development Bank). 2005. *Vision 1440 AH (2010).* Jeddah.
Ismail, Abdul Ghafar. 2011. "The Theory of Islamic Banking: Look Back to the Original Idea." *Journal of Islamic Banking and Finance (JIBEF)* 7, no. 3 (July–Sept): 9–22.

Khan, M.M., and M.I. Bhatti. 2008. "Islamic Banking and Finance: On Its Way to Globalization." *Managerial Finance* 34, no. 10: 708–25.

Kuhn, W.E. 1982. "The Islamic Development Bank: Performance and Prospects." *Nebraska Journal of Economics and Business* 21, no. 3: 49–63.

Mohamed, Ehab K.A. 2010. "Multidimensional Performance Measures in Islamic Banking." *Global Journal of Business Research* 4, no. 3: 47–60.

El Moussawi, Chawki, and Hassan Obeid. 2010. "Evaluating the Productive Efficiency of Islamic Banking in the GCC: A Non Parametric Approach." *International Journal of Finance and Economics* 53: 178–90.

Pappas, Vasileios, and Marwan Izzeldin. 2011. *Determinants of Survival in Islamic Banks.* Working paper, Department of Economics, Lancaster University Management School.

Rashwan, M.H. 2012. "How Did Listed Islamic and Traditional Banks Perform, Pre and Post the 2008 Financial Crisis?" *Journal of Appplied Finance and Banking* 2, no. 2: 149–75.

Sharif, Z.M. 2006. "Islamic Finance in Australia." *Islamic Finance News* 3, no. 14: 11–12.

al-Tamimi, Hussein A.H. 2010. "Factors Influencing Performance of the UAE Islamic and Conventional National Banks." *Global Journal of Business Research* 4, no. 2.

el-Tiby, Amr M., and Wafik M. Grais. 2015. *Islamic Finance and Economic Development.* Hoboken, NJ: Wiley.

World Bank. 2010. *Doing Business.* http://www.doingbusiness.org/reports/global-reports/doing-business-2010/

———. 2012. "GNI Per Capita." *World Atlas.* http://data.worldbank.org/data-catalog/GNI-per-capita-Atlas-and-PPP-table

Zarqa, M.A. 1983. "Stability in an Interest-free Islamic Economy: A Note." *Pakistan Journal of Applied Economics* 11, no. 2: 181–88.

Zubairu, Umaru M., Olalekan B. Sakariyau, and Chetubo K. Dauda. 2012. "Evaluation of Social Reporting Practices of Islamic Banks in Saudi Arabia." *Electronic Journal of Business Ethics and Organization Studies* 17, no. 1.

7 Olives: The Taste of Lebanon with a 'Twist'

Manar El-Batrawy and Aliaa Bassiouny

Introduction

In a quaint café in Beirut, Lebanon, in the winter of 2007, an idea slowly simmered and developed for Ayman Shaikhun over brunch. Inspired by the warmth and hospitality of the Lebanese, he started to question the scarcity of places like this in Egypt—the absence of dining restaurants that offer delicious food and a relaxing atmosphere for casual gatherings. For many years now, he had been trying to find the perfect blend of high-quality food and casual atmosphere to hang out in with family and friends on laid-back Friday mornings. Coincidentally, he had already been pondering establishing a private business that was not quite in his comfort zone; and so came the idea of Olives, 'your everyday escape,' a place where 'delicious' and 'affordable' meet. Three years later, Olives was up and running with tremendous potential for local and global expansion.

Shaikhun is a former market researcher who strived to attain his goal of becoming a successful entrepreneur. He pursued his dreams and after years of studying and surveying the market he finally established his own firm, Food Factory. The business grew significantly from its establishment in 2010, and he was able to create a brand name in the food and beverage industry in Egypt. Despite the many challenges he faced, he managed to maintain the success of the business by his strategic decisions and efficient operations. He also managed to overcome the critical recession period Egypt underwent after the 2011 revolution and was capable of maintaining his operations through these difficult times. The business is growing slowly yet steadily and achieving a fair profit margin of 10 percent per year. Some challenges could not be overcome easily, however, such as that of future expansion locally and globally.

This case delves into the development of Olives, how it materialized and the challenges that it is now facing. The case starts with the history of Olives and an introduction about the owner. Next, the development, growth and operations of Olives through the years are examined, as well as an analysis of the financial aspects of the business. Finally, the challenges facing the business are discussed, highlighting the major obstacle, which is the expansion either organically or by the introduction of new partners and the potential for global expansion in the future.

Background

Ayman Shaikhun started his professional career over twenty years ago in the field of marketing research. His last corporate role was regional general manager of a multinational pharmaceutical company. His background in research and corporate management encouraged him to apply his business insights to his new entrepreneurial venture.

The idea of Olives was initially a joint venture between Shaikhun and another investor. As often happens in entrepreneurial projects that require a high level of risk tolerance and commitment, the partner was exited in the early stages of the start-up, but left Shaikhun alone to pursue his vision of being the number one Lebanese dining restaurant in the Middle East.

Olives was created after two years of detailed market research and analysis of the food and beverage market in Egypt. While conducting the research, Shaikhun discovered a gap in the restaurant business in Egypt that motivated him further. The upscale food and beverage market in Egypt mainly consists of high-end casual dining restaurants (American-style food), fine dining restaurants, and casual cafés. The high-end casual and fine dining restaurants in Egypt are located mainly in hotels, which, while offering high-quality gourmet cuisine, are not very appealing to most Egyptian casual diners who do not want to pay the expensive menu prices. This led to casual cafés being the typical night-out destinations for younger people due to their affordability, yet they offered low quality food. Shaikhun's idea of a casual café that offers fine, affordable dining filled an obvious gap. Olives opened its doors as an affordable, high-quality and casual Lebanese dining restaurant.

With the idea firmly in place, Shaikhun consulted a Lebanese consulting firm owned by a Lebanese chef regarding menu creation and availability of materials in Egypt. Along with the high-quality food, he would offer hookah, as most Egyptians sought places that serve it.

Start-up and Growth

Olives currently has three branches, all in Cairo. The first branch opened in November 2010, and is located in the Downtown Mall in New Cairo. The location was chosen because of the number of Egyptians moving to New Cairo (currently 1.2 million and expected to grow to 6 million when fully developed[1]) and the fact that Olives would be one of the first restaurants to open in a new mall that had been widely anticipated by New Cairo residents. Being one of the first restaurants, Olives was capable of attracting a significant number of New Cairo residents in addition to those seeking an escape from the typical overcrowded restaurants. By its first year of operations, Olives was serving an average of 3,000 customers per week. After the massive success of the first branch, Shaikhun opened another branch in City Stars Mall, located in Nasr City, to capture new customers who were perhaps unable to travel to New Cairo.

Although cannibalization is always a risk, the food and beverage market in Egypt is growing at an increasingly rapid rate. In light of that, Shaikhun saw potential in opening a third branch in Cairo Festival City (CFC) Mall, which was the new 'buzz' in town, also located in New Cairo. The decision to open in CFC was partially due to the fact that the dining business in Egypt generally depends on trends, with the 'buzz' constantly moving from one place to another. Furthermore, with the number of New Cairo residents continuously increasing and as the Downtown Mall area was becoming crowded, opening a new branch in close proximity would help cater to a larger number of customers. Shaikhun saw this more as brand equity than cannibalization, meaning that going after the new, prime location in CFC would enable Olives to strengthen its position in the market by capturing new customers. As the CFC branch has not been operating long, its level of success or failure remains unknown; however, Shaikhun is optimistic.

The question remains: why hasn't he considered opening a branch in West Cairo? That is, after all, the typical trend for entrepreneurs seeking business growth and covering unserved segments. Shaikhun looks at it differently. He believes the company is still relatively new to the business and prefers to minimize risk. Since its headquarters are in New Cairo, Shaikhun raised his concerns of managing geographically distant branches, and so came his decision to continue to expand in the same geographical area as long as there is still potential. He feels that this will enable him to leverage the resources of the back office to the nearby branches and between the branches themselves. While the idea of untapped potential could be a concern, he thought that this concern would remain even if he opened in West Cairo. Therefore, he found that capturing as many New Cairo residents and visitors as he could would be far less risky than venturing into entirely different areas such as West Cairo.

The 2011 Revolution and Its Impact on Operations

The 2011 Egyptian Revolution had a huge impact on the food and beverage market and the economy as a whole. As recorded by the Central Agency for Public Mobilization and Statistics (CAPMAS), the private food and beverage sector showed a deficit of LE46,203,000 in 2011. Hence, the question of survival of Olives during and after the revolution was of utmost importance. Due to political instability, the frequent rumors about bombings at the time, and the curfew enforced from 6 p.m. to 6 a.m., Olives had to close its doors for a couple of days. It was exceedingly difficult for Olives to operate for almost two weeks as the country was in a state of utter chaos. The suppliers were not able to deliver materials and the employees had to leave two hours before the curfew started to be able to reach their homes by 6 p.m., so the serving time was very short. There were security concerns regarding the safety of the outlet itself, with the possibility that it might be looted. It was an uphill challenge for Olives to operate under these circumstances.

Interestingly enough, Egyptians adapted to the curfew, altering their outing patterns and going out in the morning instead of at night. Olives was one of the first restaurants that reopened, two weeks after the revolution started, and with the shortage in supplies, it had a limited menu of only beverages. Frequent power cuts required them to operate on gas. Nonetheless, these efforts were highly appreciated by the customers, who were bored with being locked up in their houses and were seeking an escape.

Operations

Shaikhun believes that success stems from proper management of operations and that customer loyalty is a reflection of that success. Olives' new customers are increasing by the minute and the percentage of repeat customers is increasing too. Moreover, the establishment of the City Stars and Cairo Festival City branches has not affected the number of customers visiting the Downtown Mall branch. Shaikhun believes that the main reason behind this increase in customers is the menu.

The Menu

As mentioned earlier, creating the menu took the owner two years of research and technical consultations with Lebanese chefs. After looking at the market and understanding the eating habits and preferences of Egyptian consumers, Shaikhun came up with Olives' menu. A lot of experimentation and testing of available materials took place in the process. That part of the process took place in Lebanon, where he rented a demo restaurant, a real kitchen, and hired Lebanese chefs. He had to resolve the issue of the difference in materials availability between the two countries, and this is where the 'twist' came from. Since not all authentic Lebanese dishes would appeal to Egyptian consumers, some minor changes to the plates were made and some items added that are not necessarily Lebanese. Dishes such as *kebbanayya* that do not appeal to Egyptian tastes were excluded, and because Egyptians are known for their sweet tooth, a couple of desserts were added to the menu. All of these adjustments were made after identifying cultural differences between the Egyptians and the Lebanese. Moreover, while studying the Lebanese market, Shaikhun found out that it is not strictly traditional Lebanese. While authentic Lebanese food can be found all over Lebanon, especially in the mountains, places like downtown Beirut, where most teens and younger people hang out, offer Lebanese food in new, modernized, non-traditional ways.

Purchasing

The backbone of any successful business is quality resources, such as trustworthy suppliers, skilled labor, and state-of-the art technology. Suppliers are one of the most essential elements in the food and beverage industry, as they are integral to providing quality ingredients and raw materials. The criteria for choosing suppliers differ from one business to another. The department responsible for choosing the suppliers of Olives is the purchasing department. It contacts all potential vendors and request price quotations and samples of their product for testing it. A hired professional tests the sample and ensures that the product specifications match the department's requirements. The sample is then sent to the kitchen and tested as an ingredient in a plate. At the tasting stage, the dish is tasted by chefs and approved; it is then tested with customers and feedback is collected. After feedback collection, the purchasing department negotiates the price with selected vendors. This means that prior to the price negotiation, the sample goes through a quality control cycle, leading to correct decision-making.

Suppliers

Vendors are selected based on several parameters such as production, storage conditions, and consistency. That is, whether they can produce quantities that cover the need of the merchant store it in case of high seasonal demand. Consistency in production and reliable delivery are very important. The past experiences of other restaurants with that vendor are collected to assess their performance in delivery and in quality of the product. All of these criteria need to be fulfilled in order for the purchasing department to select a vendor as its supplier.

Labor

Challenges are present in all industries, although they differ from one industry to another. The main challenge in the food and beverage industry in Egypt is labor. It exists both for new entrants and for existing businesses. The challenge in Egypt is not the supply of labor but low productivity. Shaikhun claims that personnel are not eager about self-development. He believes that this stems from the facts that illiteracy rates are high and that workers are not interested in improving their standard of living. It was difficult for him to find non-skilled labor willing to be trained for the jobs he had to offer.

On the other hand, it was easy to determine the number of personnel he needed in his restaurant. The kitchen is divided into five sections—hot, cold, grill, bakery, and steward—with two shifts per day. The number of personnel required depends on the needs of each section. In the case of service personnel, it depends on the number of seats; each worker is assigned a number of seats during each shift. He started off with 30 workers and is now at 130 total employees.

Technology

Shaikhun's vision was the trigger for using a distinct strategy for the company's use of technology. From the beginning of his business, he was concerned with offering high quality, high standards, and great taste. He uses electronic handheld devices for taking orders instead of taking them manually, in order to decrease the room for human error and to speed up the order-taking process. The use of handheld devices also increases the personal contact between the customer and the captain (the order-taker) does not have to leave the serving space. Furthermore, this increases efficiency in the ordering system, because while the order is being taken it is instantly being processed to the kitchen. In the kitchen, orders are received at each of the five sections separately with a flashing green light for every new order and a countdown to execution. For every order, there is a predetermined time, immediately after which the customer should expect his meal to arrive. This enables the management to come up with statistics and analysis of the kitchen sections' performance, so that operational decisions can be made in the kitchen. This same technology also aids in determining stock levels, and replenishment takes place automatically.

Competitors

The existence of competitors in a market is inevitable, and success depends on how an entrepreneur leverages his resources to outperform them. Olives has a huge number of competitors for the pound spent dining out. However, there were only a few Lebanese restaurants in Egypt when Olives first started. They were either fine dining restaurants or cafés, so they posed a minor threat to Olives. This is not the case nowadays, as more Lebanese restaurants are opening and competition is increasing in the market, from two or three restaurants to around twenty. This forces Olives to work on enhancing its operations further in order to maintain its standing in the food and beverage market in Egypt.

Financial Aspects

There are three main categories of innovation that an entrepreneur may adopt: invention, extension, and duplication. Invention is the creation of a brand-new idea. Extension is when an entrepreneur modifies an already existing idea and introduces it to the market. Duplication is when an entrepreneur adds a creative touch to a replicated idea. Shaikhun categorizes Olives as an extension through which he added a 'twist' to authentic Lebanese food. He decided to be an extension of an already existing idea that was proven to be successful, rather than creating a new idea that may or may not succeed.

After modifying the product, Shaikhun needed to decide how he would finance his business. The idea of borrowing was out of the question for him, so he decided to invest his savings in starting up his restaurant. He argues that in the case of borrowing, he would be under the constraints of paying back interest and principal, while in the case of investing a portion of his own savings, the maximum he could lose would be his own money. This is consistent with his relatively high risk tolerance. His methodology for expansion was through reinvestment of profits and additional cash from his own savings to increase the working capital of the business.

Olives has been expanding from 2010 to date, which is the result of an increase in sales and profit margin.[2] It has been expanding by establishing new branches and by increasing the capacity of existing ones. This expansion is a result of an aggressive compounded average growth in sales of 40–50 percent, which yields an average profit margin of 9–10 percent per year. Although this 10 percent may appear relatively low, it is actually fairly good. The cost of goods sold (COGS) amounts to 40–45 percent of the gross revenues. Of the remaining amount (the gross profit), the ever-increasing property costs consume up to 30 percent. Sales taxes take another 10 percent, and income taxes an additional 20–24 percent (table 7.1).

Table 7.1. Olives income statement, 2013

Category	Percentage
Revenue	100%
COGS	42% (of revenue)
Gross profit	58% (of revenue)
SG&A	15% (of gross profit)
Operating expenses	7% (of gross profit)
Rent expenses	23% (of gross profit)
Depreciation	4% (of gross profit)
EBIT	9% (of gross profit)

These profits are reinvested in the business for expansion rather than changing the capital structure of the business either through borrowing from a bank or introduction of new partners. Although such a change in capital structure might result in more rapid growth and expansion, Shaikhun decided not to do this, as it is riskier than expanding gradually and organically. The motive behind not borrowing or introducing new equity was that he needed to balance between fast growth and quality growth that ensures consistency and efficiency in operations of existing branches prior to opening new ones. He also preferred having a fully-fledged management team to operate existing branches rather than introducing new partners with a different perceptions of things.

Prior to establishing his first branch, Shaikhun constructed a financial model to identify and manipulate key performance indicators drivers and to study the impact of different financial and operational variables on profitability. This aided Shaikhun in the decision-making process and in making adjustments to achieve his objective. Feedback collected from customers on a daily, weekly, and monthly basis is used to revise the business performance. Feedback on the menu items, taste, and service quality is taken into consideration to take corrective actions. Other variables, such as monitoring vendors' pricing and property costs, were critical to profitability.

Shaikhun did not hire a financial analyst but conducts the analysis himself with the help of operational management department reports. These departments are purchasing, personnel, accounting, IT, and quality control.

SWOT Analysis

In order to understand Olives' current position in the market among other competitors, the company conducted a SWOT analysis. SWOT analysis is a framework that is used to analyze a business's internal 'strengths and weaknesses and the opportunities and threats' from the surrounding environment. Since its establishment, Olives' positioning as a casual Lebanese dining restaurant was very clear and the slogan 'your everyday escape' was easily understood by the customers. Its affordability and high quality of food were recognized and highly appreciated. The second strength is Olives' consistency and significant development over the years in terms of food quality, service quality, and operations. This improvement has been an internal strength to the business and reinforces its positioning in the market. The third strength is the perfect blend of high-quality food and service with the right price point. The management comes up with competitive pricing rather than charging high prices for high-quality food.

Like many other businesses in Egypt, Olives lacks skilled labor. The absence of competent labor disrupts the process of providing high service quality in branches, and the lack of a solid managerial structure results in the absence of internal succession in managerial positions. In time, experienced people will be promoted internally, which will eventually strengthen the organizational structure. Additionally, the absence of sustainable and consistent suppliers is a weakness for the business. This involves not only reliable delivery of the product, but also the consistency of the quality that was previously agreed upon. Another weakness is specifically in the Downtown Mall branch, where the infrastructure and the utilities are a little out of date. In order to improve these facilities, the branch would have to shut down for a period of time, which would significantly affect the branch's profit margin.

To quote Shaikhun's own words about the opportunities in the food and beverage market, "the sky is the limit." The first opportunity is expansion in West Cairo, after capturing the maximum number of customers in East Cairo with its three already established branches. Another opportunity is the continuous growth of the food and beverage market in Egypt in general, which would allow the business to grow as well. The fact that customers are becoming more and more selective when it comes to the quality of food and services presents an opportunity too, as it results in acknowledgment of the effort exerted in Olives' operations.

The absence of skilled labor poses a threat to the business as well as being an internal weakness in Olives' operations. The lack of a competent workforce is a threat to the consistency of the business operations. Moreover, since Shaikhun's methodology of running a business is more about teamwork than a one-man show, this lack of professionals and skilled labor

Figure 7.1. SWOT analysis

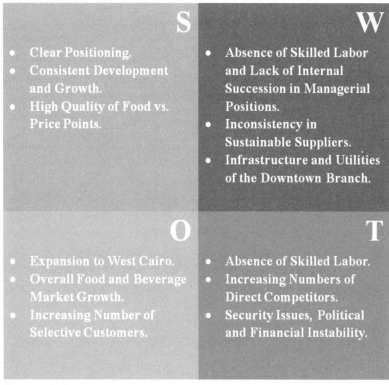

(Source: author)

negatively affects the business. Another threat is the rising number of direct competitors in the food and beverage market. Political, financial, and security issues pose a threat to Olives' operations because of the instability in the market and the country as a whole and the fear that further recession may result in numerous restaurants exiting the market.

Porter's Force Field Analysis

This theoretical framework analyzes the food and beverage industry in Egypt and the performance of Olives' strategy among other key players with an assessment of the driving and restraining forces that exist in the market. The five influential forces that shape competition in the market are the bargaining power of suppliers, rivalry among existing competitors, the bargaining power of buyers, the threat of substitutes, and the threat of new entrants. Suppliers' bargaining power is relatively low as Olives' criteria for selection are rather rigorous. This gives Olives the ability to dictate the price of the products purchased from these suppliers. Also, Olives' customers are becoming more and more selective when it comes to food preference and quality. Their power has increased due to the rising numbers of competitors entering the market and the availability of other service providers of the same product, Lebanese food.

Figure 7.2. Porter's force field analysis

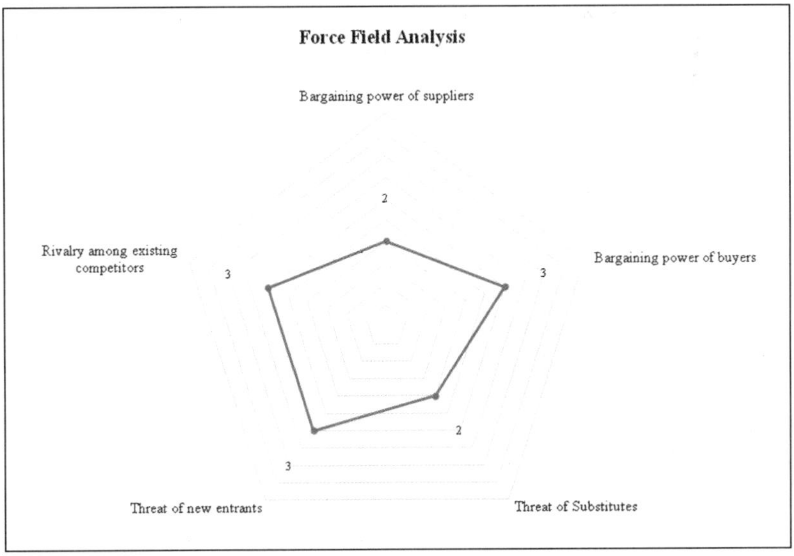

(Source: author)

Olives' substitutes are Italian, Thai, Chinese, and Oriental restaurants, among others. The threat of these substitutes is relatively low since Lebanese cuisine appeals to customers because of the close similarity in ingredients or even dishes between it and Egyptian cuisine. Barriers to entry to the food and beverage market in Egypt are relatively low, though, allowing other players with sufficient capital to enter the market and provide the same type of cuisine. This exerts pressure on Olives and requires continuous development in operations to maintain or even increase the number of customers captured. Players in the food and beverage market in Egypt are all competing for the pound spent on dining out, and since the number of Olives' competitors is continuously increasing, the competitive rivalry is relatively high.

Challenges

No entrepreneur should overlook the existence of the challenges inherent in the business. One of the major challenges Shaikhun faced was finding trained and skilled labor to work in his business. He can overcome this issue either through training unskilled workers himself or using a recruitment firm to select skilled ones.

Another challenge that Shaikhun faced was the lack of transparency in local regulations and the discrepancies of business laws in Egypt. An example of this is the fact that Shaikhun was not informed of a particular law until he received a fine because he had breached it. Another example was the lack of information regarding the authorities that he needed to contact prior to establishing his own business. Correcting this problem would require a reform of the governmental system in order to facilitate and encourage entrepreneurs to establish new businesses.

Maintaining standards and customer satisfaction is the core of any business. A successful entrepreneur is required to monitor the performance of his business continuously, especially in the food and beverage market, which can be extremely time-consuming. In order for Shaikhun to maintain his customers' high level of satisfaction he needs to collect their feedback continuously; this can only be done through dealing with customers in person. It requires high levels of energy, dedication, and sacrifice. Since this kind of business cannot be operated remotely, he needs to always stay on his toes and exert more effort than in most other industries. Another problem is that weekends and holidays are peak business times, so he needs to sacrifice his leisure time in order to monitor performance personally. Another way of dealing with this issue would be to hire trained, trustworthy professional managers, who monitor business operations efficiently.

Additionally, food and outings in the Middle East, especially in Egypt, are very trendy. The competitive landscape constantly changes and this requires the entrepreneur to be alert to frequent fluctuations in the market. The entrepreneur has to fully understand the change in consumers' behavior and outing patterns while already managing a hectic operation.

As for financial challenges, there are many that might hinder expansion. These challenges can be the lack of supplier receipts that result in higher costs and, in turn, higher taxes. This can be corrected through enforcing binding contracts and rules on the business's suppliers. Ever-increasing property costs are a problem, especially now that property owners are enforcing protocols that mandate profit sharing in addition to rent. Since property costs amount to a significant portion of business expenses, Shaikhun can solve this issue through long-term contracts. Another financial challenge is the need for the installation of advanced, state-of-the-art technology solutions to help manage existing branches and potential expansion. The need for technology solutions adds overhead costs that are not necessarily covered by revenues.

All of these challenges accompany any start-up with varying magnitude. The biggest dilemma that persists for Shaikhun, however, is future local and global expansion and whether he will expand organically or with the introduction of new partners. In order for Shaikhun to expand, he has a long road ahead of him, full of challenges and areas for improvement.

Conclusion

Markets evolve in the Middle East and North Africa region as a result of continuously expanding businesses opportunities. It is believed that successful entrepreneurs are the key driver for booming markets. Ayman Shaikhun, founder and CEO of the Food Factory enterprise, pursued his dream of entering the food and beverage market and creating his own brand name. After surveying local and international restaurants for more than two years, he was able to identify an appealing cuisine for Egyptian consumers. Olives, 'your everyday escape,' is a Lebanese restaurant that has been successful and growing for several years now. Shaikhun started out with one branch in Downtown Mall, New Cairo, at the end of 2010, and opened another two branches despite the ongoing political and financial instability in Egypt.

With a background in market research, Shaikhun could easily recognize the first obstacle ahead of him, which was selecting the cuisine that most suits consumers' tastes. After analyzing the Egyptian market, he classified it into two main categories (casual cafés and high-end casual dining). He evaluated the demand for various cuisines before choosing Lebanese cuisine. He sought to establish a middle category of restaurant that falls between casual cafés and high-end casual restaurants. This would be a place where people can spend time and socialize, as in the case of cafés, while being served high-quality food, as in the case of high-end casual dining restaurants. Filling the gap between casual cafés and high-end casual restaurants was by no means the only dilemma he faced before opening Olives. The method of financing the project was problematic in the first place, as were obstacles along the way for future expansion, whether locally or globally. The answer to the question of whether Olives has the capability to expand remains unknown, yet promising.

Notes

1 New Cities of Egypt e-portal, http://www.newcities.gov.eg/know_cities/New_Cairo/(1).aspx
2 Since Olives is a privately held business, actual numbers are kept confidential, while financial ratios are published as an indication of financial performance.

8 Birthing Pains: The Issues Faced by Start-ups in the United Arab Emirates

Ashraf A. Mahate and Sanjai K. Parahoo

Development of the Business Idea

It was 2 p.m. on a Thursday afternoon and Abdulla stared at his laptop as he had done for most of the day, wondering what to do. In a half-hour it would be the end of the day and the start of the weekend. Abdulla was wondering what had happened since he returned to the United Arab Emirates (UAE) after completing his undergraduate degree at one of the most prestigious universities in the United States. Time had flown by and now he was married with a young family, and of course with that came responsibilities and obligations. When Abdulla returned to the UAE all those many years ago, he, like many other UAE nationals, joined the public sector.[1] At the time the public sector was the largest recruiter of UAE national graduates and provided them with considerable opportunities to grow, acquire skills, and develop their capabilities.[2] Abdulla quickly moved up the ranks and by the age of thirty-two he held a very senior position in government. Despite reaching such a high level in a relatively short space of time, Abdulla was not satisfied with his accomplishments; there was something missing in his life but he could not quite put his finger on it.

Abdulla did not realize that all his colleagues had left the building and he was still staring at the blank laptop. The cleaners walked in and out of his office without his knowing what was happening. Suddenly he was awoken simultaneously by the call to prayer and by the realization of what he needed to do. It seemed as if it were a divine guidance that he should develop his entrepreneurial ability and venture into the world of commerce. Abdulla had come from a business family and felt that he had the necessary will and drive. Even when he was at university he decided that he would set up a small enterprise to fund his education, a venture that was very successful and that he only closed in order to return to the UAE. Throughout his working life Abdulla sought to establish his own business where he could make all the decisions and reap the rewards, but it was never the right time to do it. 'Was now the right time?' he asked himself.

That evening Abdulla discussed his idea of establishing a business venture with his family. Although they were very supportive, the obvious question of what business to establish arose. Abdulla had not thought about this; he just felt he possessed business skills and acumen to become successful in any area. He had shown that, coming from an IT background, he had become successful in areas as diverse as customer service and government administration. Also, not only had Abdulla completed an MBA, but he was also the top of his class. The MBA course was good for acquiring skills and knowledge but it could not help in the fundamental question of what kind of business to establish.

For many entrepreneurs the question of what type of business to start is the most difficult one. For some entrepreneurs it is easier, as they tend to branch out from their existing activities, where they already have the sector knowledge and an established network. As he was coming from the public sector, this option was not available to Abdulla. All weekend Abdulla was preoccupied with developing a business idea or at least selecting possible industry sectors. He knew that he enjoyed IT, but was this a market he should enter? He also enjoyed football and was on various sports committees. Perhaps this could be an option; he could establish a sports academy. With increased public interest in sports this could be a possibility. Just then Abdulla noticed a headline in the newspaper. At the time Dubai was bidding to host the Expo 2020 event, and the article stated that during the six-month period the emirate was expecting over 33 million tourists. More importantly, if Dubai were successful in its bid to host the Expo, it was forecast that over 300,000 direct and one million indirect jobs would be created.[3] This set Abdulla to thinking that perhaps he should target an Expo 2020-related business, but the event was seven years down the line. He needed to create a business that would be financially feasible not only leading up to 2020 but also for the period after the Expo.

Even if he could not establish a business that was directly related to the Expo 2020 he could at least develop a business that could benefit from it. The fact that stuck in Abdulla's mind was that 33 million visitors would be visiting Dubai over a six-month period. If this was true, the greatest opportunity in business might lie in the tourism sector. A quick search on the Internet showed that Dubai received about 9.96 million tourists in 2012 and this trend was increasing even during the international financial crisis.[4] An Internet search also revealed that not only were the tourist numbers increasing but so was their length of stay in Dubai. Key areas of demand in the tourism sector were in accommodation, related services such as providing excursions and tours, and leisure services.[5] All these areas of activity are highly related to seasonal factors, however. In a region such as Dubai the weather becomes unfavorable from April to the end of September. Abdulla felt that it would be rather risky to set up a business that was so dependent on tourist numbers. He did, however, feel that he needed to capitalize on the booming tourism industry and to link it to the lifestyles of long-term residents in the emirate. In this way there would be business activity throughout the year.

Food Service as the Solution

That night Abdulla and his family were having dinner at a recently opened restaurant in Dubai Mall, the largest shopping mall in the world and a favorite with tourists and residents. He looked around and realized how busy the restaurant was even though it was relatively new. Was the restaurant busy because it was new and people were trying it out, or was there something to the food service sector? After dinner Abdulla walked around Dubai Mall and saw that the restaurants and coffee shops were truly busy. That's it, he thought to himself; he had found the ideal business sector to enter. It must be the restaurants or coffee shops. He had no experience of ever working in the food service sector, though; all he had done was eat in restaurants and coffee shops.

Over the next few days Abdulla decided to carry out some initial research into the sector. His research showed that fast food and cafés in the UAE saw increased growth in terms of both number of stores and sales (see tables 8.1 and 8.2). This was due in part to the cultural dynamics of the country, where consumers demanded quick and convenient meal solutions. At the same time, Islamic customs meant that bars and pubs, which are common in Western societies, are not the norm in the UAE. Instead, socializing tends to be carried out over non-alcoholic beverages in the evening in coffee shops.[6] The weather also plays an important part in consumer behavior, with home delivery being a popular method of consumption. In fact, food service providers use home delivery to increase sales and a number of stores rely on this medium for the bulk of their sales. The importance of home delivery prompted well-known stores such as McDonald's to offer this option. Soon Abdulla was able to find the number of food service stores along with the number of transactions and market value of the sector. This was very important information that would allow him to produce financial projections for his own venture. (see table 8.1). Also, the research showed that the market was growing over the last five years (see table 8.2).

Table 8.1. Units, transactions, and value of sales in consumer food service, UAE, 2007–12

	2007	2008	2009	2010	2011	2012
Number of food service stores	4,377	4,619	4,776	5,021	5,260	5,602
Transactions (million)	406.9	448.9	468.4	496.9	535.0	584.3
Sales (million AED)	16,709.20	20,269.20	21,452.90	23,768.70	26,690.80	29,634.80

Source: Euromonitor International, 2013.

Table 8.2. Units, transactions, and value of sales in consumer food service, % growth, UAE, 2007–12

	Compound Annual Growth Rate 2007–12
Units	28.0
Transactions	43.6
Sales	77.4

Source: Euromonitor International, 2013.

Abdulla's research also showed that the food service sector was dominated by international brands such as Kuwait Food Co. (Americana) with KFC and Pizza Hut, and Emirates Fast Food Co. with McDonald's (see table 8.3). These brands tended to cross the income and cultural market segmentation and appeal to a mass market. Franchising was also important because many malls in the country were conservative and preferred a well-tried and tested format rather than taking a risk on a new idea. In fact, in the UAE, franchising in the food and beverage sector outweighs domestically created concepts.[7] Furthermore, the extremely hot weather in the country means that shopping malls are an important venue for

Table 8.3. Global brand shares in chained consumer food service: % food service value, 2009–12

Brand	Global Owner	2009	2010	2011	2012
KFC	Yum Brands	7.4	7.4	7.5	7.5
McDonald's	McDonald's Corp	7.8	7.6	7.0	6.9
Pizza Hut	Yum Brands	5.2	5.0	4.8	4.3
Subway	Doctor's Associates	3.1	3.0	4.0	4.1
Burger King	Burger King	4.1	3.8	3.6	3.6
Baskin Robbins	Baskin Robbins	3.1	3.6	3.5	3.5
Hatam	Al Khaja Group	2.6	2.6	2.6	2.7
Chili's	Brinker International	2.9	2.8	2.6	2.3
Paul	Holder Group	1.9	2.0	2.0	2.2
Hardee's	CKE Restaurants	2.7	2.5	2.4	2.1
Starbucks	Starbucks Corp	2.2	2.1	2.0	2.0
Costa Coffee	Whitbread Plc	1.9	1.8	1.8	1.8
Al Farooj Fresh	Al-Islami	1.5	1.5	1.3	1.4
Dunkin' Donuts	Dunkin' Donuts	1.5	1.4	1.5	1.3
Tim Hortons	Tim Hortons	—	—	0.0	1.3
Wendy's	Wendy's	—	—	0.9	1.2
Domino's Pizza	Domino's Pizza	1.2	1.1	1.1	1.2
TGI Fridays	Carlson	1.0	1.1	1.1	1.1
Papa John's	Papa John's	0.4	0.7	1.0	1.0
Cold Stone Creamery	Kahala Group	0.7	0.8	0.8	1.0
Just Falafel	Just Falafel	0.1	0.2	0.6	0.9
Zaatar w Zeit	Cravia UAE	0.9	0.9	0.9	0.8
Fatburger	Fog Cutter Capital Group	0.3	0.4	0.5	0.8
Burger Fuel	Burger Fuel Worldwide	—	0.1	0.4	0.7
Johnny Rockets	Johnny Rockets	0.1	0.2	0.4	0.6
London Fish and Chips	London Fish and Chips	0.2	0.3	0.4	0.6
The Meat Company	Food Fund Management	0.5	0.7	0.6	0.6
Cinnabon	Focus Brands	0.4	0.4	0.4	0.5
Caribou Coffee	Caribou Coffee	0.6	0.6	0.6	0.5
Al Hallab	Hallab Restaurant & Ptns	0.4	0.6	0.5	0.5
Others		45.4	44.8	43.2	41.0
Total		100.0	100.0	100.0	100.0

Source: Euromonitor International, 2013

individuals and families to spend leisure time. Malls not only have shops and restaurants but also other leisure facilities such as cinemas, sports activities, libraries, arts centers, theaters, and art galleries. Thus, it is conceivable that people go to shopping malls not simply to carry out purchases but to spend a day or a large part of it carrying out leisure activities. Shopping malls are therefore of the greatest significance for consumer food service: studies show that almost all visitors to a shopping mall typically purchase at least one consumer food service drink, snack, or meal. Abdulla carefully tabulated the results of his research so that he could better understand their implications (see tables 8.1, 8.2, 8.4, 8.5, and 8.6).

After a detailed analysis of these findings, three things became obvious to Abdulla. First, he would have to establish his food service operation in a shopping mall rather than as a stand-alone unit. Second, if he were to establish it in a shopping mall he would need to have an international franchise, as mall operators were reluctant to allow new and untried formats and concepts. Third, his limited expertise in the food service sector suggested that he should focus on an area that required little in the way of complicated cooking and food preparation. This meant that the focus of his activities would need to be on beverages. His research had shown that if he were to focus on drinks, then a café was the most likely option (see table 8.4). After an exhaustive research exercise he decided that he would establish an internationally franchised coffee shop because of the marketing importance of chains (see table 8.5).

**Table 8.4. Sales in consumer food service versus drinks: %
Foodservice Value, UAE, 2012**

	Food	Drink	Total
100% home delivery/takeaway	90.0	10.0	100.0
Cafés/bars	39.2	60.8	100.0
Full-service restaurants	67.8	32.2	100.0
Fast food	71.8	28.2	100.0
Self-service cafeterias	90.0	10.0	100.0
Street stalls/kiosks	87.0	13.0	100.0
Consumer food service	58.8	41.2	100.0

Source: Euromonitor International, 2013.

Table 8.5. Consumer food service, independent versus. chained: units/outlets, UAE, 2012

	Independent	Chained	Total
100% home delivery/takeaway	—	120	120
Cafés/bars	1,227	345	1,572
Full-service restaurants	1,242	321	1,563
Fast food	1,227	1,001	2,228
Self-service cafeterias	4	4	8
Street stalls/kiosks	111	—	111
Pizza	41	214	255
Consumer food service	3,811	1,791	5,602

Source: Euromonitor International, 2013.

Table 8.6. Sales in consumer food service by location: % food service value, UAE, 2007–12

	2007	2008	2009	2010	2011	2012
Leisure	3.5	3.5	3.6	3.7	3.8	3.8
Lodging	26.4	28.1	28.1	28.2	28.2	28.1
Retail	40.2	40.8	41.4	42.1	42.8	43.7
Travel	2.4	2.6	2.7	2.7	2.8	2.9
Stand-alone	27.5	25.1	24.2	23.3	22.4	21.5

Source: Euromonitor International, 2013.

Franchising Route

If Abdulla were to franchise, which food sector brand should he choose, especially as the UAE already had all the major international chains? Was franchising even a sure way to business success? He understood that with a franchise he would obtain a recognized and established brand name, image, concept, and positioning. This was important in the UAE, with residents from over 130 countries and growing tourist numbers. Also, he felt that the franchiser would provide someone like Abdulla, who had no experience in the food sector, with training and would help him in setting up the business with regular mentoring and advice.[8] Talking to local banks, Abdulla became aware that they were more likely to lend money to a franchise with a good reputation. There were also disadvantages to think of, such as that costs would be higher than if he were to set up the operation. As a franchisee, he would have to fund the initial costs of buying the franchise and continuing royalties. In addition he would be tied into an arrangement where he might have to buy products from the franchiser. Further, the franchise agreement might have restrictions on how he could run the business. Then there was the possibility that the franchiser might go out of business, or change the way it does things.[9] He was also aware of situations in franchising where other franchisees gave the brand a bad reputation. Of course with reduced risk he might not generate vast profits. Weighing up the advantages and disadvantages, Abdulla felt that the consumer behavior trends in the UAE, along with the requirements of shopping malls and his lack of experience, meant that a franchise operation was in fact the best option (see tables 8.1 through 8.6).

Now the question was which franchise he should select and what factors he should consider. With little help or guidance, Abdulla decided that he would carry out further research to better understand the market. He knew that the current market was well supplied by North American and European brands and formats. What the market lacked was diversity of brands and tastes. He needed a coffee shop with a new format that would allow him to differentiate his business from the competitors. Abdulla knew from his experience in the government of Dubai that there were non-Western brands in the coffee and restaurant business but they were not always successful. He needed an international franchise that allowed him to be different while maintaining a connection with the cultural eating and drinking habits of the country. He knew that as far as hot beverages were concerned, the local favorites such as 'kahrak' tea and coffee (strong, creamy, fragrant brewed tea or coffee of Indian origin) were just as popular as Western espressos, cappuccinos, and so on. The problem with the kahrak tea and coffee shops was that they were stand-alone units and not branded. Abdulla knew that kahrak tea and coffee was not limited to the Gulf region and was present in Asia. He researched major coffee franchises in Asia and compiled a list of the ones that appealed to him.

Investigating Singaporean coffee franchises
Abdulla found that the top three coffee brands on his list were from Singapore, so he decided to visit the country. But first he carried out further research to learn about the brands and the potential market for them in the UAE. The first thing Abdulla found was that there were four direct non-stop flights between Singapore and the UAE each day, and many more with a single stop. The high frequency of flights between the two countries implied a strong and steady two-way traffic between the two

countries. This meant that a Singaporean brand would be easily recognized by UAE residents as well as appealing to tourists from Singapore. Data from the Dubai Tourism and Commercial Marketing Department (DTCM) showed that in 2012 there were 35,000 tourists from Singapore to Dubai. A decade earlier the number of Singaporean tourists to Dubai was only a quarter of the 2012 number.[10] Secondly, some of the brands on his list had already expanded into other Asian countries, which gave them additional market recognition. Prior to his trip to Singapore Abdulla needed to communicate with the concerned companies. He wrote to six companies in Singapore and four replied requesting his company profile. Abdulla had not thought of writing a company profile as he had not even registered his company. Abdulla decided to write back to the companies with his own profile and explain what he wanted to do. Only two companies were interested in talking to someone who did not have a corporate profile or any real experience of running a commercial enterprise.

Abdulla wondered if he should have formed a partnership with someone with some commercial business experience or at least knowledge of running a food service operation. He wondered whether he should wait and find appropriate partners or build his own team and then produce a profile. Would this help him in obtaining a better franchise, or as a first-time entrepreneur would the large franchisers still ignore him? He thought about this and then decided that he still had two companies that were interested in his proposal. It would not hurt for him to meet with these two companies and perhaps investigate the other companies on his list further. Abdulla arranged to meet the two companies on his list in Singapore. Prior to his meetings, he visited a number of their branches in Singapore. He felt that his opinion should not be clouded by testing just one store; he needed to visit several of them. As a result of his market visits Abdulla was better able to understand the products, their branding and positioning, the market served, and the corporate culture of each brand. This was an important consideration for him as his brand needed to be flexible enough to be adaptable to the cultural sensitivities, behaviors, and needs of consumers in the UAE. He knew from his earlier research that some franchisees were extremely inflexible and as a result tended to have a mixed level of international success.

Meeting with Ya Kun Kaya Toast management
Before meeting Ya Kun Kaya Toast, Abdulla had a meeting with another franchiser, who was extremely polite and informative about their products

and culture. Abdulla thought that it might succeed in the UAE but something made him unsure. His instinct was not in favor of going ahead with this first brand. Was it to do with the experiences that he had while he was in their coffee shops or was it that he felt he did not develop an initial chemistry with the company? He was not sure but he was convinced that he did not have the same feelings of incertitude when he went to meet Mark Leo, the CEO of Ya Kun Kaya Toast.

Abdulla first came across Ya Kun Kaya Toast (Ya Kun), a chain of cafés selling toast products made from kaya (a jam-based product) and coffee, during a family holiday a few years earlier. Ya Kun had very humble beginnings. It was established by Loi Ah Koon in 1944 and it remained a family operation until the end of the 1990s. Today Ya Kun has over fifty outlets that are franchised in over seven countries, with a very strong Singaporean theme. The Ya Kun coffee stores are described as 'a retro ambience with wooden tables and stools, Chinese calligraphy of the company name, posters about their history, traditional methods of preparing food and customer service reflecting Chinese family values.'[11] Unlike its competitors, Ya Kun has a limited menu that is focused around kaya, which is a jam-based product. More recently, Ya Kun has established a family version of its cafés, which sell a wider range of meals but are very Asian in focus and thus highly differentiated from its competitors. Ya Kun also differs from its competitors in pricing its products 'slightly higher than those of its local competitors but lower than prices of comparable products at Western coffeehouse chains operating in Singapore.'[12]

According to the World Intellectual Property Organization (WIPO), Ya Kun has made over fifteen national trademark applications with the Intellectual Property Office of Singapore for its 'Ya Kun' name, the 'Ya Kun Kaya Toast Coffee Stall, Since 1944' slogan, various posters representing the company's history, and the names of popular products such as 'Toastwich.' It has also submitted an international application under the Madrid system for its name and slogan. Ya Kun trademark applications are made either under the company name of Ya Kun (S) Pte. Ltd. or its international franchising arm, Ya Kun International Pte. Ltd. The official licensee for use of the Ya Kun trademark abroad is Ya Kun International.[13]

One of the key themes of Ya Kun is its nostalgic ambience; thus all the outlets have the same posters showing scenes of bygone days and the history of Ya Kun. Abdulla wondered whether such historical references would appeal to a Middle Eastern audience or if he would need to educate customers about their meaning. Abdulla knew that there were a large number of Asians in Dubai and felt that in time this meaning would spread through word of mouth. According to WIPO, Ya Kun's posters are protected in Singapore by trademark applications, as are its manuals and other materials used in its franchise system. No such application had been made in the UAE, and Abdulla wondered if this would need to be done. He was aware that in the UAE the market is highly competitive, and there is no reason why another firm could not copy the posters if he did not protect them. He thought he would worry about it once he signed the franchise agreement. Then he remembered that throughout his visits to Singapore he could not find a kaya jam like that of Ya Kun. The reason was that Ya Kun's intellectual property strategy is based on protecting, through trade secrets, its kaya jam recipe, which is manufactured in a separate, family-owned facility by staff comprising only family members. The senior management ensures that this recipe is not disclosed to outsiders, along with the mix of various types of coffee beans that are used in its stores, which give its coffee a special aroma and flavor.

Abdulla had a very successful set of meetings with Mark and his team and was then provided with the franchise package that gives franchisees the rights to operate the Ya Kun Kaya Toast concept, use of Ya Kun's distinctive identity and trademark, initial and ongoing support, free exchange of new ideas, research and development (R&D), marketing and public relations support, and a steady supply of official Ya Kun products.[14]

Establishing Ya Kun Kaya Toast in the UAE

Soon after meeting Mark Leo, Abdulla decided that Ya Kun was the brand for him. He set about inviting the company's team to the UAE so that he could show them possible locations and introduce them to the country. Mark and his team had received other requests from potential franchisees in the UAE, but they felt that they wanted to work with a small and eager partner rather than a large company where Ya Kun would simply be one more brand in their stable. Over a few months Abdulla and the Ya Kun team communicated extensively, which produced a well-researched market feasibility study. The benefit of working with a franchise company was that they were able to share their knowledge with Abdulla. For their franchise operations they had a template for a feasibility study with benchmark calculations for their operations in Singapore. In this way franchisees could easily see how their market dynamics, costs, and revenues compared to the Singapore operations. Also, their in-house software allowed Abdulla to conduct scenario analysis, which helped in developing his business plan.

The experience of Ya Kun in a number of different countries also meant that they were aware of the different risks and the various solutions available. One such process was registering the intellectual property with the appropriate authorities in the UAE.

Armed with a comprehensive market feasibility study and business plan, Abdulla was able to sign a franchising agreement with Ya Kun. Until then, Ya Kun had been assisting Abdulla on the basis of a letter of intent in the absence of a formal agreement. Now with almost all his questions answered Abdulla felt he was ready to formally embark on this business relationship. In the process he became more familiar with the company and their team. At the same time Ya Kun was able to understand the UAE market and the potential that it offered. This was also the time when serious discussions had to take place with regard to the initial cost of the franchise and the royalties that needed to be paid.

From Abdulla's perspective, he had to decide in what regions he wanted the master franchise—whether it would be just Dubai, the UAE, or the entire Gulf Cooperation Countries (GCC) region. The more expansion in the region, the more the initial cost increased. Abdulla knew that he could not limit himself to just Dubai; it would have to be at least the entire UAE. The next question was if he should obtain the GCC master franchise. He knew that brands that were successful in the UAE did well in other GCC countries. Did he have adequate resources to manage operations in all six GCC countries, though? Should he concentrate on making Ya Kun a success in the UAE first, and then perhaps consider other GCC countries? But if he did this, might somebody else obtain the franchising rights?

Abdulla knew that, since his was the first franchise in the GCC, if there were a serious request for another GCC country the Ya Kun team would give him first right of refusal. He decided to opt for the UAE master franchise, agreeing to the standard terms offered by Ya Kun. The franchiser argued that they could not change the terms in each country and that royalty rates were the same for all countries. What was negotiable was the initial cost of the master franchise. Even this was set to a certain extent, as the fixed costs of setup in terms of legal costs, company visits, and so on was the same. After some discussion, Abdulla and the Ya Kun team agreed on the terms and signed the franchise agreement.

With the franchise agreement firmly signed, and armed with a comprehensive feasibility study as well as a five-year business plan, Abdulla set about deciding on the next set of key issues. He knew that he could ask his family to help him raise the necessary financing. Abdulla felt that he wanted to make this venture his own, however, and that would mean using his own funds. Over the years that Abdulla had worked in government he had saved some money, but it was not going to be sufficient. He decided to visit his local bank to borrow funds. Like all financial institutions, they simply did not understand how to lend to start-ups with no track record. Abdulla's bank required him to put up collateral before they would give him the necessary financing. He decided to offer his home as collateral. He knew that this type of funding would only be sufficient for the start-up capital he needed; if he were to expand, he would need to find alternative sources of financing.

The next question was whether Abdulla should resign from his government position or employ a manager to look after the coffee shop. Abdulla thought for a while and decided that he needed to ensure that he had a stable income to repay the bank loan. He could not risk losing the family home and the shame this would bring. He felt that the only viable option was for him to employ a full-time manager. This would increase his costs but it would bring vital food and beverage experience that he lacked. In setting up his business Abdulla did not require any sponsor, as was the case with expatriate investors (see table 8.7). As a UAE national Abdulla also had the freedom of using any type of business structure he felt was appropriate. The next issue was to identify a suitable location. Coming from a large and well-known family, Abdulla knew that he could use influence, or, in the phrase that is used in the UAE, 'wasta,' to find suitable locations.[15] Abdulla had studied ethics as part of his MBA program and knew that such use of influence was common in business in the Gulf countries. However, he felt that he should start his business on the most ethical model, and submit his application to the shopping malls like any other firm.

Abdulla's ethical behavior paid off and he soon found an ideal location in Ibn Battuta Mall, a well-known shopping mall in Dubai. The next step was for him to agree to the standard terms of the mall. He soon realized that shopping malls in Dubai had considerable power, especially given the large waiting list, and there was little he could do in terms of negotiating prices or payment terms. Abdulla signed the lease for three years, which was the minimum period, and paid one year's rent in advance with the deposit. Next he obtained the business license, which in Dubai was relatively easy (see table 8.8). Soon after obtaining the business license, Abdulla asked Mark and his team to come to Dubai and help him design the store and draft the tender document for the refit. Abdulla and Mark together chose the company that did the refit and the store was delivered back to Abdulla on schedule.

Table 8.7. Conditions for starting a business in Dubai

UAE National
United Arab Emirates nationals can operate all commercial, professional, and industrial activities through the following legal structures: • individual establishment • limited/joint liability company • private/public shareholding company • civil business company
GCC National
GCC nationals can conduct business activities through any of the following legal structures: • individual establishment • limited liability company composed of two or more GCC nationals may establish a Limited Liability firm • private/public shareholding company, where three or more GCC nationals establish a private shareholding company to practice a specific commercial activity. However, if there are one or more partners who are not GCC nationals, then one or more UAE national partner(s) is/are required, with a shareholding of 51 percent of the paid-up capital. For example, a GCC partner and a foreign partner must have at least one partner who is a United Arab Emirates national. • civil business company, where two or more GCC nationals can establish a civil business company to practice a specific profession without a local services agent. However, if there are any partners who are not GCC nationals, a local services agent who is a UAE national must be appointed and/or included as a partner.
Non UAE or GCC National
Nationals of other Arab or foreign countries may carry on economic activities through any of the following structures: • An individual establishment can be established to practice any professional activity, by appointing a local services agent who is a UAE national selected from among the partners or outside party. • A limited liability company can be established to carry on any commercial or industrial activity, including one or more UAE partners whose shareholding is 51 percent of the paid-up capital. • A private shareholding company can be established to carry on any commercial or industrial activity, including one or more UAE national partners whose shareholding is 51 percent of the paid-up capital. • A civil business company can be established by two or more persons to practice a profession, provided that a Local Services Agent who is a UAE national is appointed or included as a partner. The main differences being the number of participating parties allowed within each business venture's structure, who may or may not be a Local Services Agents or who may be a partner respectively.

Source: Dubai Chamber of Commerce and Industry, 2012

Table 8.8. Procedures, time, and costs of business set-up

Procedure	Time required to complete	Costs
Submit the company registration application and the proposed company name to the Dubai Department of Economic Development (DED) at one of the office desks in the relevant DED agencies.	1 day	AED100 fee for the initial approval
Notarize the company's Memorandum of Association in DED at the foreign direct investment office.	1 day	0.25 percent of the capital (for 3 copies of the Memorandum of Association), AED5 for each page of the additional copy
File company documents with the DED and obtain trade license and the Dubai Chamber of Commerce and Industry (DCCI) membership at the DED and the DCCI respectively.	6 days	5 percent of the value of the lease agreement + AED1,000–3,000 waste fees + AED480 for company registration + AED500 fees for signboard approval + AED 1,200 for Chamber of Commerce membership registration.
Make a name board (describe what this is) when the company receives clearance on the use of the office premises. Prepare a name board in English and Arabic. The office premises will then be inspected by the fire and civil defense authorities and by the DED Licensing Department.	2 days	AED1,000
Apply for establishment card at the Ministry of Labor.	1 day	AED2,000
Register native workers with the Ministry of Labor.	1 day	no charge
Register native workers with the General Authority for Pension and Social Security.	1 day	no charge

Source: http://www.doingbusiness.org/data/exploreeconomies/united-arab-emirates

Market positioning and store locations

With a store location in hand, Abdulla and Mark were ready to develop their market positioning strategy. Mark knew that in Singapore Ya Kun was positioned to be both relevant and significant to its target market. It was relevant in that it was priced above local competitors and significant because it was cheaper than Western brands. In doing so Ya Kun was positioning itself to target an affluent group who were regular visitors to its stores. A successful part of its positioning strategy was the very nature of its products as well as its premises. In terms of products in Singapore, Ya Kun is known for its kaya jam and products based around this. In the UAE kaya jam is new, but kahrak tea and coffee are well known. However, kahrak tea and coffee are also associated with lower-end, cafeteria-type establishments frequented by laborers. To position Ya Kun as a kahrak tea and coffee shop would demean the product range. At the same time the coffee shop market was highly congested, with almost all international brands and many regional ones represented. Therefore, market positioning had to ensure that Ya Kun was differentiated from its competitors in terms of product attributes such as the size, shape, color, lettering, and art of a store, the product packaging, and precise quality and taste specifications. In terms of intangible attributes, Ya Kun had to be positioned as a premier Asian experience that is exciting, entertaining, and different. As Mark said to Abdulla, "If consumers want a muffin or croissant they can go to our competitors. If they want an Asian indulgence they come to Ya Kun."

Abdulla recalled from his MBA class that, according to Porter's competitive strategy theory, the least defensible competitive strategy is being 'stuck in the middle.' Companies that are neither price competitive nor offer a highly differentiated product or service experience cannot have a long-term sustained competitive advantage. The danger of a differentiated strategy, meanwhile, is that it can lead toward creating a niche market. Such a categorization would severely hinder Abdulla's ambitions of expanding the number of stores in the UAE. After careful thought, Abdulla and Mark felt that their market positioning had to be differentiated from their competitors' to the extent that customers recognized the difference but not to the point that it became a marginal purchase. Also, their market positioning implied that they could not have stand-alone locations, which were traditionally associated with non-branded lower priced outlets. Ya Kun stores had to be in prime locations within shopping malls where they would be visible to their target audience. Abdulla's earlier research had also shown that there was a higher probability of a food service outlet making a profit in a shopping mall, for two reasons. First, a typical shopping mall such as the Mall of the Emirates has about half a million visitors each week. The high footfall in a mall implies a greater probability that the target audience will try Ya Kun. Second, the UAE lifestyle suggests that it is easier for consumers to purchase from a store in a mall due to parking convenience, ease of reach, weather convenience, and the like. From a market positioning viewpoint, an outlet in a mall would allow Ya Kun to implement a broad differentiation strategy on a par with the international coffee shops present in the UAE.

Developing a customer-centric model and product development
Abdulla had worked in customer service and had initiated several programs to help retailers improve their customer service. He knew that if he were to make a success of his business venture he would need to ensure that the coffee shop was customer-centric. For this he would need to know what the customers appreciate, tolerate, and actively dislike so as to focus attention on the areas that matter. He recalled from his prior training that he needed to think like a customer. At the same time the employees should act as consultants who feed information to him. In this way the company would get continuous feedback, both positive and negative, about the customer experience. Abdulla also recalled the example of a restaurant in one of the training courses that he arranged, where the owner understood the plight of customers who wanted to escape the 40-degree Celsius heat and offered them complimentary ice-cold water with lemon slices on the counter and a cold towel to refresh themselves. Abdulla pondered two questions: Was this the way to go? If he started such a system would he be able to maintain it?

One problem that Abdulla faced was that his employees had a limited educational background and had not graduated from hospitality training institution. He needed to train them extensively so that they could perform at the desired level. In Dubai trained staff are highly prized, however, and they are poached by competitors for a very small increase in salary. Abdulla questioned whether training itself was the only solution to increase customer satisfaction, but he was not sure what else was needed.

Another problem that Abdulla faced was that his product range was very Asian and largely untested in Dubai. Would it be accepted in the UAE? Abdulla studied Ya Kun's menu and wondered what needed to be done, if anything, for it to be successful. The Asian character of the food had certain advantages, in that any customer wanting Asian food and coffee should immediately think of Ya Kun. Yet if he were to follow this strategy he would narrow his customers into a niche market. The UAE is a very complex market where eating habits do not follow a standard pattern. This meant that Abdulla would need to offer conventional meals and beverages as well as Asian ones. But would this create 'noise' and dilute his product positioning? Abdulla was not sure what to do, but he knew that he needed to test the market and see what would work and what would not in terms of product mix.

Financial and inventory management
Financial management is one of the most important aspects of any business and there is little room for mistakes in this area. Abdulla had some experience and basic financial skills that perhaps most start-ups do not have. He knew that no financial management could solve a restaurant's financial problems if they result from inadequate sales. The key was to increase revenue but at the same time ensure that fixed costs were a reasonable percentage of sales; otherwise the enterprise ran the risk of not being profitable. As he had never managed a coffee shop he was not sure what the reasonable level of fixed costs should be. Abdulla also knew that in food-related business he had to minimize wastage because he made money not only from what was sold but also what was not sold. Abdulla thought of how he could predict the amount of sandwiches, meals, and beverages that would be consumed, or if there were a way to ensure that wastage was very limited. Most of his meals had to be prepared in advance so the waiting time was limited, but that might result in high wastage. He thought that perhaps if he were running high with inventory for the day he could always give away free samples as a marketing move, but that would still imply a cost.

As a small business Abdulla could not afford to recruit an accountant, even though he knew the importance of a well-organized and well-implemented accounting system. He knew that he did not have sufficient business to warrant the high cost of an accountant or even a bookkeeper. He chose to purchase accounting software and maintain the accounts himself, at least until he achieved a sufficient level of business growth. In the absence of an accountant, he had to implement his own financial controls in order to ensure that staff did not abuse the trust given to them. Abdulla knew from his friends who had established businesses that there were issues with staff taking money from sales. Even with sophisticated cash machines, staff had learned that they could cancel a transaction and pocket the cash. Also, he had heard stories of staff taking inventory home or even selling it to other stores. As a small business he could not afford any of this and he had to make sure that such losses did not take place. Like most stores, Abdulla installed a video surveillance system so that he could monitor his staff, and with the technology available he could view the coffee shop from his mobile phone or laptop. Abdulla still wondered if this was enough to stop any of the problems he had heard about.

Almost One Year Later: Models for Managing Expansion

Almost one year after establishing the coffee shop, Abdulla was extremely pleased that his first coffee shop was successful, in that he started to make a profit and he had a regular base of customers. Abdulla was right in thinking that the huge mix of nationalities in the UAE would mean that an Asian format would appeal to his target audience. He smiled with the conviction of a job well done when his customers asked him when he would be opening in a location closer to them.

Abdulla did have a vision of a chain of locations throughout the UAE. His initial business plan considered the possibility of sub-franchises, because some his customers might wish to get into the format. With a chain he would need his own capital and a team of managers to oversee the locations. More important, he would need a large capital base to open the additional locations. With a franchise model, though, he could receive a franchise fee and franchisees would provide their own capital to open their locations. In such a format his costs would be limited to developing a sub-franchise manual and management system, while if he established his own chain he would need to do a lot more. Yet full ownership would mean that he would still have control over his company and not need to rely on the efforts of sub-franchisees. He was aware that sub-franchising did not always work, as most of these owners were new entrepreneurs with little experience of running a business, let alone a food service operation. There would be a considerable need for hand-holding, and even then he could not guarantee that the sub-franchisees would perform according to his expectations. He could limit the risks by setting up a centralized kitchen that produced the meals and sandwiches, thereby ensuring consistency of product.

Even though Abdulla favored the sub-franchising model, he somehow also saw the merits of a fully-owned operation, although he did not have sufficient capital. He considered whether he should accept the offer that two of his friends had made, of putting capital into his business in return for equity. The additional capital would allow him to establish another two or three stores but the tradeoff would be a huge reduction in his shareholding. Also, bringing in partners would have issues of its own. Which was the right expansion model to follow, he wondered.

Notes

1 There are only 20,000 Emiratis in the private sector out of a population of more than four million people, compared with 225,000 Emiratis in the public sector. Source: http://www.thenational.ae/uae/uae-narrows-holiday-gaps-between-private-and-public-sectors-to-woo-emiratis, 14 November 2013.
2 The Minister of Labor commented that "job security, regulated working hours and higher wages are among the reasons Emiratis prefer the public sector." Source: http://www.thenational.ae/uae/uae-narrows-holiday-gaps-between-private-and-public-sectors-to-woo-emiratis, 14 November 2013.
3 http://gulfnews.com/business/economy/dubai-expo-2020-how-5-key-industries-will-benefit-1.1314613. 5 April 2014.
4 http://www.dubaitourism.ae/sites/default/files/hotelstat/2012_Guests_by_Month.pdf
5 http://www.dubaitourism.ae/sites/default/files/hotelstat/2006-07-Dubai-Visitor-Survey-2006.pdf
6 http://arabicwithoutwalls.ucdavis.edu/aww/chapter9/didyouknow.html
7 https://www.zawya.com/story/Franchising_in_the_UAE-ZAWYA20130521073135/
8 http://www.franchoice.com/franchise-information-guide/franchise-buying-steps/should-you-buy-a-franchise
9 http://franchises.businessmart.com/advantages-disadvantages-of-owning-a-franchise.php
10 http://www.dubaitourism.ae/sites/default/files/hotelstat/2003-2012_Guests_by_Nationality.pdf
11 www.yakun.com
12 www.yakun.com
13 www.wipo.org
14 www.yakun.com
15 'Wasta' or 'wasata' is an Arabic word that is commonly used in the Gulf countries to imply the use of influence or connections in order to obtain something.

References

Blanchflower, D.G., and A. Oswald. 1998. "What Makes an Entrepreneur?" *Journal of Labor Economics* 16, no. 1 (January 1998): 26–60.
Casadesus-Masanell, R., and J.E. Ricart. 2011. "How to Design a Winning Business Model." *Harvard Business Review* 89, no. 1: 100–107.
Euromonitor International. 2013. *Consumer Foodservice in the United Arab Emirates.* Euromonitor International.

Dubai Chamber of Commerce and Industry. 2012. *Starting a Business in Dubai.* http://www.dubaichamber.com/documents/Starting%20a%20Business%20in%20 Dubai.pdf

Gillis W., and G.J. Castrogiovanni. 2012. "The Franchising Business Model: An Entrepreneurial Growth Alternative." *International Entrepreneurship Management Journal* 8: 75–98.

Lovelock, C. and J Witz. 2011. *Services Marketing.* 7th ed. Harlow, UK: Pearson Education.

Martin, D.M. 2009. "The Entrepreneurial Marketing Mix." *Qualitative Market Research: An International Journal* 12, no. 4: 391–403.

Porter, M.E. 2008. "The Five Competitive Forces that Shape Strategy." *Harvard Business Review* 86, no. 1: 25–40.

Thompson Jr., A.A., M. Peteraf, A.J. Strickland, and J.E. Gamble. 2012. *Crafting and Executing Strategy: Text and Readings.* 20th ed. New York, USA, McGraw-Hill/Irwin

9 A Hybrid Agribusiness Value Chain: The Case of a Horticulture Social Enterprise in Minya, Egypt

Nagwan Ibrahim, Farage Lashin, and Ali H. Awni

Background

Despite economic growth in Egypt over the few years prior to the January 25 Revolution, living conditions for average Egyptian citizens did not improve. Poverty and unemployment were on the rise, and annual inflation was increasing at a rate that could not be matched by the increase in wages. Upper Egypt, the region in the south of Egypt from Beni Sweif to Aswan, lags behind the rest of Egypt in terms of development. The region has a high poverty rate, low per capita income, and high unemployment compared to the rest of the country. Investments in Upper Egypt account for only 13 percent of total investments in Egypt even though the region's 22 million inhabitants account for 27 percent of Egypt's total population. The total workforce of Upper Egypt is 5.7 million, 1.2 million of whom are women. This gap in development is illustrated by table 9.1 (UNDP, 2005), which compares the average economic indicators of Egypt to those of Upper Egypt.

Table 9.1. Economic indicators, Egypt as a whole vs. Upper Egypt

Indicator	Egypt	Upper Egypt
Poverty rate	20.0%	34.0%
Illiteracy rate	34.3%	43.5%

Source: UNDP, 2005

127

The government of Egypt realizes the potential of Upper Egypt, with its surplus of labor and huge areas of land, as an opportunity that is not exploited yet. Furthermore, it is clear that the current situation in Upper Egypt could be a major contributor to instability and produce a breeding ground for extremism if not improved. In the last few years the Egyptian government started to intensify its efforts to narrow the gap between Upper Egypt and the rest of the country. This is evident from the incentives given to industrial investments in the region and the major infrastructure projects to facilitate investments in the region.

Agriculture remains a major source of income and employment for many families in Upper Egypt. The ownership of agricultural land is very fragmented, and farmers suffer from the poor infrastructure.

Minya, one of the governorates of Upper Egypt (shaded area in the map in fig. 9.1), is mainly an agrarian society where over 80 percent of the workforce are directly or indirectly involved in agriculture-related activities. Traditionally most of the agricultural products are sold to traders and middlemen from other governorates who add no value to the supply chain; their only focus is on maximizing their profits. Upper Egypt, including Minya, has not had its fair share of development for the past five decades. The local communities were therefore deprived of the basic rights of obtaining decent employment opportunities; unemployment was high, and families were barely managing to cover their basic needs and were living in very poor conditions. Furthermore, there was a general culture of mistrust among the farmers due to the exploitative practices of traders and middlemen who supplied exporters and agricultural crop manufacturers.

Under these circumstances, social entrepreneurs (Bornstein and Davis 2010) can play a critical role in developing businesses that have a positive social impact on their community. "A social entrepreneur is an agent of change in society: pioneer of innovations that benefit humanity" (Davidsson 1989, 210). Social entrepreneurs bring systemic change by addressing not only the problems they directly confront, but also the cause of those problems. Moreover, social entrepreneurs are generally more effective than international NGOs in addressing the root causes, because they are better integrated into the societies they serve and know the specific needs of their beneficiaries (Bender et al. 1990). Social entrepreneurs continually seek out and realize ways for positive social change in areas where others only see challenges, and in ways that have sustained impacts over the long term. Social entrepreneurs instinctively find reasons why things

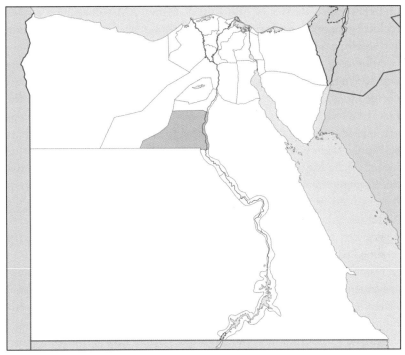

Fig. 9.1. Map of Egypt, with Minya highlighted
source: Nordwest (Own work) [CC-BY-SA-3.0 (http://creativecommons.org/licenses/
by-sa/3.0)], via Wikimedia Commons

can happen. They are dedicated to changing the systems and patterns of society to create community value and meet critical unmet social needs and social problems.

Our case is centered around Ahmed Dakrouri as a successful social entrepreneur. Dakrouri is the creator of a Comprehensive Agricultural System that empowers farmers and revitalizes impoverished regions of rural Egypt, for which he was recognized by Ashoka (a global network of social entrepreneurs) as a social entrepreneur and Ashoka Fellow in 2007. Dakrouri's family has a long history in serving Minya. It started in 1924, after Egypt's 1923 constitution. His great-grandfather was a member of the Egyptian parliament. After three generations, his father was the last to serve, continuing until 1995, after which he was active in local community service. In 1995, Dakrouri's father established the Abu Korkas, Minya, Association (AMA) for Economic, Social and Environmental Development to provide socioeconomic development services in the underdeveloped district of Abu Korkas, Minya. AMA developed a track record by supporting the establishment of 184 small, successful production and service projects between 1996 and 2003.

After over fifteen years in executive management in construction, engineering, contracting, and consulting services firms, Ahmed Dakrouri decided to go into private business. He developed two major ventures: the first was a tourist resort project (1994–2002), and the second was the preparation and packaging of meat cuts to international standards and practices to supply leading hotels and restaurants in Egypt (2002–2005). In the meantime, he was exploring opportunities to develop an export operation for horticultural produce (since late 2003). In August 2004, Dakrouri's father passed away. Dakrouri made the conscious decision to take over the NGO his father had formed and to continue the family heritage of serving the community. He became the chairman of AMA, which was shortly renamed to Green Economy Development Association (GEDA).

Dakrouri's vision was to develop Minya's farmers' and growers' skills and practices so that they could supply safe and quality crops to the local market and for export, thus driving sustainable development of local communities and improving overall standards of living. To do this, Dakrouri developed the Agricultural Product Value Chain (APVC) model to connect farmers to markets, to assist them to produce to market requirements, and to cut out the middlemen who were seizing most of the profit with no contribution to the skills and caliber development of small farmers. The model calls for aggregating groups of small farmers in Minya into cooperative formations, providing them with intelligence on market opportunities and technical assistance on what crops to grow and how best to grow those crops, and enabling them to participate in export activities and to get better prices for their products. Dakrouri's vision was to empower farmers and enable them to make their own decisions collectively through the development of a comprehensive agricultural supply system that produces export quality crops that meet market requirements. By doing so, new job opportunities would be created, improving farmers' income and allowing them to acquire new skills. The initiative provides the grower community in Minya access to local and international markets, as an alternative marketing channel.

Attempting to change the modus operandi in the market meant encountering resistance. The fiercest resistance was from the benefactors of the current system, the traders and the middlemen. The hardest change, though, was changing the mindset of the farmers from trade-based relations to a collaborative long-term mindset. In order for the model to succeed, Dakrouri had to gain the trust of the small farmers through consistently being there and demonstrating the benefits they would gain by joining this program. Dakrouri's program involved the transformation of the existing agricultural system by implementing modern agricultural practices to increase productivity during growing and harvesting.

There are two major learning points to be found in this case. The first is the approach that Ahmed Dakrouri used as a social entreprenuer, capitalizing on his family name and long heritage of service, and the steps he followed to gain the trust of small farmers to encourage them to cooperate within the new value chain concept. The second is the unique 'hybrid value chain' model (a term coined by Ashoka) that is used, with a mix of social enterprises, regular business enterprises, and NGOs, to enable small farmers from the 'base of the pyramid' to organize, obtain technical assistance and finance, and cooperate to export quality agricultural products.

The Entrepreneur

The social entrepreneur is an agent for change. It is critical to study the main factors affecting his life and his choice of becoming a social entrepreneur. Many factors had affected Dakrouri throughout his life and contributed to his decisions and actions as social upbringing, family heritage, education, and work experiences. Dakrouri is an Egyptian social entrepreneur descended from a political family with a long history of public service. Since 1924, Dakrouri's family has served in the Egyptian parliament with the aim of serving their community in Upper Egypt.

Factors affecting the entrepreneur

Despite living in Cairo and his constant travels, Dakrouri visited his family's hometown of Minya regularly to spend time with his father and other family members. Dakrouri was strongly influenced by his father, whom he regarded as a role model. His father was a political figure in Egypt who actively served the local community and who established the AMA. The AMA supported the establishment of 184 small, successful production and service projects, for a total disbursement of LE4.4 million between 1996 and 2003, through a tripartite agreement with the Social Fund Development (SFD) of Egypt, and with 100 percent payback (principal and interest) to the SFD.

Education is one of the variables that affect social entrepreneurs' behavior. Coming from a prosperous family, Dakrouri was well educated. He studied in an English school in Cairo and then in an elementary school in North Carolina, in the United States, when his father was completing his Ph.D. He graduated from Cairo University in 1978 with a bachelor's degree in civil engineering, and obtained a master's degree in project management from the Massachusetts Institute of Technology (MIT) in 1982. Dakrouri completed several technical and managerial training programs, the most notable of which was a nine-month work training program in project, logistics, and finance management in Germany between 1985 and 1986, which he was able to tailor to suit his needs and gain the skills that he could apply in Egypt.

Dakrouri started his work experience during his university summer vacations, during which he worked in construction in Europe. After graduation in 1978, he worked in Egypt as a site engineer in construction projects, supervising the work of a team of engineers and representing the owner's consulting office. Through this role Dakrouri experienced the problems associated with managing projects and developed a passion for improving project development. This drove him to formally study project management at MIT. Upon completion of his master's degree, Dakrouri became the business development manager of the Montasser Contracting and Reconstruction Company in Egypt between 1983 and 1984. Dakrouri continued to develop his project management skills through formal training in Germany in 1985–86, and was thereafter appointed as a project manager in Dar Al Handasah, which is one of the top ten ENR 500 (Engineering News Review) companies worldwide. Through this role Dakrouri managed projects locally and internationally. This experience further broadened his skill set, allowing him to take on roles in industries not related to his core discipline. In 1989, Dakrouri became a management consultant for TEAM International, where he participated in the analysis and design of organizational structures and the development of technical and administrative systems for industrial, services, and construction projects across the Middle East. In a career shift, Dakrouri joined National Aerospace Geotopological Management, a major air and space surveying services firm, in 1991 as a vice president for planning. He was responsible for the development of large country-scale and government-level consulting projects providing air and space surveying services to governments in the Middle East and Africa.

After over fifteen years in executive management, Dakrouri decided to go into private business. In 1994, he became partner and managing director of SADARA Development, Inc., his first major private project.

As CEO, he led a team to develop the concept of an integrated holiday destination resort with an 'Entertainment Attraction Center' theme-based approach. Another shift in Dakrouri's work experience was in 2002, when he decided to move into the food industry, and set up El Masry Modern Food Industries (MMFI), partnering with a technical expert in this field to develop a brand and market leadership in the preparation and packaging of meat cuts to international standards and practices. Building on an existing meat processing facility owned by his partner, MMFI became the market quality leader in less than six months, providing quality services and supplies to the leading food retail businesses (hotels and restaurants) in Egypt. Dakrouri's role was developing the business, opening new markets, and managing the client interface setting up systems for product coding, client relations, and requisitions.

Two years after he joined this business there were obvious signs of food shortages in the world, which assured Dakrouri that he was in the right business. Dakrouri started exploring the field of agricultural exports through which he could build on Egypt's year-round agriculture-friendly climate, contribute to the local economy, and close market gaps. He traveled to Europe frequently to identify opportunities and client demand. This proved to be an invaluable starting point for Dakrouri's development initiatives, as described below.

The shift to social entrepreneurship

In May 2004, Dakrouri's father, who had spent his life in public service, passed away. Dakrouri made the conscious decision to take over the NGO his father had formed in order to continue the family heritage of serving the community. He became the chairman of the AMA in August 2004. Dakrouri was able to apply the project management and leadership skill he acquired throughout his career to restructure AMA to serve the community more effectively.

The vision

Dakrouri's vision was to develop Minya's farmers' and growers' skills so that they became a base to supply export-quality crops to Europe, thus driving sustainable development in the local community and improving the overall standard of living. Minya was already a major internal supplier of agricultural products to other governorates, such as Asyut, Beni Suef, and Fayoum, which then re-export these products through traders and merchants and gain all the profit. Dakrouri's APVC model connected the farmers directly to markets—local and international—and cut out the middlemen. Dakrouri's vision was to empower farmers and enable them to make their own decisions as a group through the development of a comprehensive agricultural system that produces export quality crops that meet market requirements. This would create job opportunities, improve the income of the farmers, and allow them to acquire new skills.

Implementation

To implement the APVC model, Dakrouri had to follow certain systematic steps to gain the trust of farmers and families, bearing in mind that Minya had had no major development in the past five decades. This developed a culture of ignorance, and led the farmers to seek primarily easy access to money without consideration of their future development. This mentality meant that some farmers would decline to join the program, as they were not interested in the new approach and were resistant to change.

Building trust

There was a general culture of mistrust in the agricultural system due to the fact that small farmers, at the base of the pyramid upstream of the supply chain, and exporters and agricultural crop manufacturers, at the receiving end of the local supply chain, relied on middlemen and traders who add no value to the supply chain and cause market imbalances and distortions. Growers were always questioning what they would gain out of working with a particular individual or organization.

Another cultural challenge Dakrouri faced was the high number of women who were in agriculture to support their families. In some villages of Minya, up to 70 percent of households were provided for by women who were the primary, and sometimes the sole, breadwinner. Due to the local conservative culture and in order to reach this very important portion of the population, Dakrouri developed a second major initiative, namely, the Productive Village/Productive Community program, and created a team of young, educated women to reach out and support women in the target communities. They applied the same approach Dakrouri used and explained the services they could offer and the new skills that women could acquire by joining this program. This would in turn help them provide better support to their families and add economic value to society. In addition to these working women joining the program, they were also able to set an example of leadership in their respective communities and relay the message to their husbands and other men within their families as to how to respond to socioeconomic challenges and the changes that were taking place in rural Egypt, and to build wider support for their initiatives.

Dakrouri leveraged his good family heritage and its history of public service to encourage farmers and their families to join the program. He explained the services that his organization can offer and that his approach is based on a new development culture that promotes collaboration and is not the conventional trade-based approach. Dakrouri felt a great responsibility to make this project succeed due to the faith that people had in him and his family.

From the outset and throughout the process, he engaged members of the local communities in continuous dialogue, led by three counselors. The counselors helped him to better understand the nuances of the local culture and how to approach local people in their own language. These three young men were from the same village, in their thirties, and well connected with the people. They were also close to Dakrouri and he was able to interact with them, take their advice, and listen to their opinions. They had three different characters that complemented one other: the first was a police officer with a very high intellect; the second was in the finance sector, so he was a great asset in the area of investment and projects development; and the third was working in agriculture and had a great talent for dealing with others. As they were from the village they were knowledgeable about the local culture, with which Dakrouri was not very familiar at first. He explained his program ideas to them and asked the three to help translate them to the locals in a way that was in line with the local culture.

Dakrouri needed a working team to help him achieve his goal. His key measure for selecting the team was people with ethics and a good reputation. He was not looking for experienced people in this field, as the experience would come through participation in the program. Dakrouri was not looking for employees, but for partners, individuals who were willing to work hard and assume responsibility. Due to the huge challenge of trying to adapt new cultivation techniques and convincing the farmers to buy into it, there was always going to be a huge workload. He counted on his mini advisory council, his three friends, to nominate people to work with him, as he was not yet close to the people there. In the countryside, it is very easy to find information about people just by knowing their full names and villages, as the networks and families are closely intertwined. His mini advisory council had lots of contacts, and between them they were able to nominate people who met Dakrouri's criteria. Dakrouri did not intervene in the execution of the work, but provided the necessary support and management coaching, so as to empower his team and allow them to develop. His goal was to set up an institution that relied on a solid team foundation and not on individuals. This was a major change from the prevalent individualistic approach. Dakrouri tried to set up a work system, an organization, and an information system to support this model. He provided on-the-job training for the team. A few months after starting the model, everyone knew their roles and exact responsibilities and was able to contribute.

Most of the people who started working with Dakrouri over seven years ago are still there, which means they have one of the highest retention rates in Minya. This is considered a success of the working methods and the selection criteria of the team. Seven out of the ten men who initially joined the campaign are still part of the team, and of the women, the only reason any of them left was due to marriage or having children.

The Hybrid Value Chain Model

The mission of the APVC system is to improve agricultural practice, develop agricultural value chains, provide new and improved job opportunities in Minya—an area of high unemployment—and improve the income of small farmers within the system. It is a business solution to fight poverty and deprivation in Minya.

The objectives of the value chain as identified by Dakrouri (2014) are:

- Assist growers to produce crops to market specifications for the local market and for export.
- Empower the growers to choose what crops they would like to produce by providing access to market information.
- Provide the grower community in Upper Egypt access to local and international markets (an alternative marketing channel).
- Create a trade environment based on collaboration and promote the idea that competition should be international, not local; that trade takes place between supply systems; and that Egypt as a whole is a supply system.
- Promote food safety and the consumers' right to safe food.
- Invest in the growers through awareness-raising campaigns, training, and field technical support (extension service), to take the grower from subsistence to sustainable agriculture.

The model created is a reproducible, comprehensive agriculture production, processing, and supply (PPS) system and value chain. *Production* focuses on empowering farmers, developing their capacities, addressing their needs, and providing them with knowledge and services to produce to market requirements. *Processing* involves the addition of value and improving the quality of the product, and ensuring that it complies with client requirements. *Supply* focuses on marketing and responding to specific local and international market demands.

Dakrouri's program involved the transformation of the existing agricultural system by implementing modern agricultural practices to increase productivity during growing and harvesting. A number of enterprises and associations were formed to establish this integrated agricultural supply system under the umbrella of the "Horticulture of Upper Egypt Production-Processing-Supply" (HUE PPS) system (fig. 9.2). It includes AgriServ, a farm and logistics service company established to serve agricultural growers and farmers, in addition to other complementing and supporting entities. It provides a range of business-related services to complement the community development services offered by GEDA and the West Hills Farmers Association (WHFA), which include:

- Market studies and marketing services for outsourcing the production of agricultural produce to food processing and export companies, to meet their exact requirements, thus creating value.
- Pre-contracting with farmers, either directly or through their Farmer Associations (FAs) or WHFA.
- Managing farmer–buyer relationships, from studying needs to settling of final accounts; obtaining product specifications and negotiating preferential terms and prices; securing quality seeds on credit for the farmers and placing guarantees for the seeds on behalf of the farmers; and managing accounts and payment logistics with the client and farmers.
- Securing logistics for the farmers, from receiving and transporting the seeds to their distribution among contracted farmers; then, harvest and post-harvest management, including timing of harvest; sorting, packing, collection, weighing, loading and transport to client facilities; and receiving and testing at client facility.

HUE PPS is an integrated social enterprise model. While GEDA is the civil services organization (CSO) providing social services to the farmers, WHFA is a farmers' association (likewise a CSO) intended to provide value-added services to the farmers to support and develop the PPS system. WHFA provides and develops crop production programs, training, and extension services to farmers to implement those programs and to promote

Fig. 9.2. APVC main stakeholders

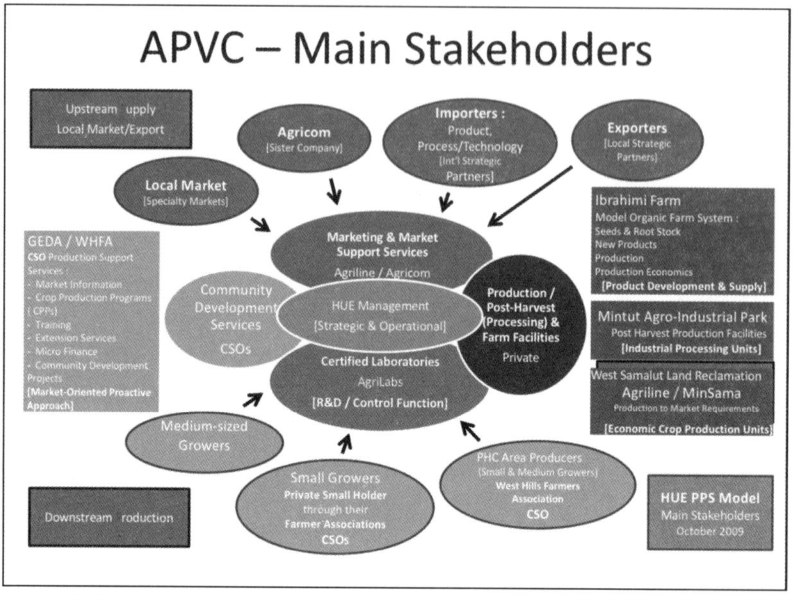

Source: GEDA

production of clean and organic products. This is a model for contract farming which has been successfully implemented in other countries to supply crops in accordance with market specifications. WHFA utilizes a board of farmers to monitor the activities of other farmers, to create a collaborative environment, and to spread a new agricultural and development culture. Mobilizing farmers and connecting them to local and international markets is laying the foundation for improved use of land and water, an increase in farmers' income, and eventually the creation of enough wealth to allow for more social and economic investment in the region.

Under the HUE PPS system, farmers were able to concentrate more on the agriculture process, its development, and the improvement of production techniques, which in turn would allow them to cultivate larger land areas. Logistics are handled by the other supporting organizations. The resulting process has considerably increased profits for the farmers as well as improved their living conditions in a sustainable way. With world market fluctuations, prices of agricultural products have been negatively impacted in some cases. The focus on providing value to only specific crops was not adequate and the PPS system revenues have been severely affected, hence Dakrouri's services are expanding in the areas of saving on production costs and protecting farmers' improved incomes from these world market influences.

The revenues coming out of the APVC programs' economic activity were at first inadequate; starting costs were high and the revenue from the economic activities did not come immediately. Therefore Dakrouri had to bear many expenses himself until reaching the break-even point. Ashoka contributed to cover some of the expenses in the beginning. Ashoka also helped Dakrouri connect with other social entrepreneurs through the forum they provide.

Farmers in the HUE PPS network receive market information and guidance, pre-marketing and preferential prices for crops, crop production programs and cost reduction, new and improved seeds and rootstock, technical advice in the production of 'safe food' according to global GAP and organic certification, training and skills development, extension services (through a team of experts, agronomists, and area supervisors), alternative natural and organic products for plant nutrients and for pest control, harvest and post-harvest management, logistics management (land provision and preparation; seed distribution; extension services; field technical support for sorting, packing, weighing, and receiving from growers; transport, delivery, weighing, and testing at the factory; accounts; and payment to growers), and microfinance for the production cycle. Buyers would receive products to their exact requirements. This reliable service enforces the trust among all the stakeholders, thus solidifying the sustainability of the system.

A big part of Dakrouri's undertaking involves delivering services to the farmers—at a small fraction of their actual costs—to upgrade them and change their mindset. Those services are direly needed in the long term to enable small famers to participate in the commercial value chain in a sustainable manner, and much needed in the short term as well, to enable them to survive and fulfill their commerical and social obligations. One way to handle this situation is to keep the commerical issues with commercial entities, and to create non-governmental organizations (NGOs), or CSOs as they are now called, to handle the social services. CSOs may rely on membership dues, government support, large corporate donations, or other sources of donations to sustain their mission. Another contribution of the CSOs is creating a solid network of small farmers, nurturing trust among them, and creating a sense of common purpose among all members. These value chains are refered to as Hybrid Value Chains by Ashoka (for example, Drayton and Budninich 2010; Hammond 2010).

Fig. 9.3. The business model's main units

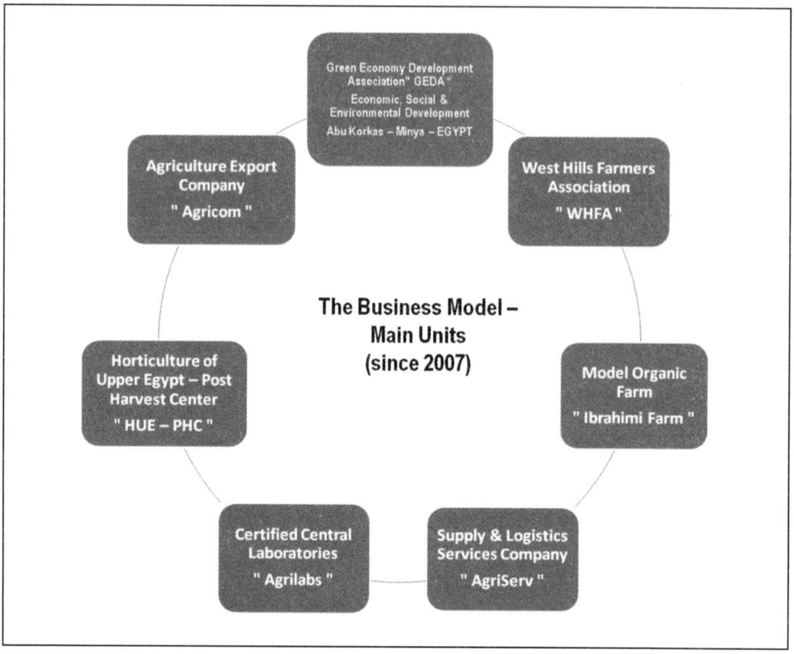

Source: GEDA

Figure 9.3 depicts the main units of the business model. Both GEDA and WHFA are CSOs, with a clear social mission and objectives, while the remaining units are business entities delivering mainly commercial services and driven mainly by commerical objectives.

Challenges

The effect of establishing this model is to turn a group of small and medium landowners into a truly cooperative enterprising society, with clear win–win objectives for all. Restoring trust between stakeholders is essential for switching a model from traditional 'trade-based' arm's-length relationships to a true cooperative, long-term enterprise. Upgrading is critical to enable the small farmers to produce up to the specification and requirements of the target markets, both local and export. This upgrading and the associated development come with an initial cost, until the farmer achieves the necessary capability. A major challenge is always how to finance these upgrading costs. Dakrouri tried to appeal to the corporate social responsibility (CSR) initiatives of large companies in the agribusiness value chain.

His experience thus far is that he cannot rely on CSR to plan for sustainable upgrading. What has worked in the past for APVC is participating in programs such as UNIDO's (United Nations Industrial Development Organization) Pro-Poor Horticulture Value Chain for Upper Egypt, and other programs for upgrading medicinal and aromatic agriculture. Egypt is in dire need of more direct funding programs to promote new forms of cooperatives in agriculture as tools of social justice and to combat poverty. Dakrouri and other businessmen are lobbying the government to influence the new cooperative law that was expected in 2014. This law should create a more conducive legal and legislative environment for APVC operations. Dakrouri has also gone on study missions to the Netherlands to study their cooperatives experience.

Attempting to change the current modus operandi in the agribusiness value chain in Upper Egypt puts Dakrouri on a direct collision course with the main current beneficiaries of the system: the traders and the middlemen. Unlike APVC, traders and middlemen are cash-rich, work with large volumes, and source from a larger base, including other governorates besides Minya. Therefore, traders and middlemen have more options and alternatives to choose from, which make them less vulnerable than APVC to delays or disruptions in the value chain. They have engaged in a price war to tempt contracted farmers not to work with APVC. Furthermore, they resorted to spreading negative rumors to dissuade farmers from collaborating with APVC.

APVC uses contact farming with farmers' associations of small or medium farmers as the mechanism to get legally binding agreements with stakeholders. The contracts are for a required volume of a crop with certain specifications and with a guaranteed price, which help small farmers mitigate the risk of price fluctuations. It is a constant struggle to convince the farmers of the value of the guaranteed prices. Small farmers appreciate it when prices fall, but complain when prices go up. One approach to convince small farmers to participate in APVC is to show them the key performance indicators that APVC uses, to see how much the small grower would gain by working with APVC. This gain results from working with farmers to improve productivity during cultivation and harvest, and enhancing capacity to produce quality crops that garner better prices.

Conclusions and the Way Forward

The APVC model is an interesting example of a collaborative approach that forms strategic alliances between farmers in Minya and other stakeholders to combat poverty and to move farmers from subsistence agriculture to sustainable agriculture. The design illustrates how to exploit the complementarities between civil society organizations (CSOs) and private commercial companies to form partnerships for success, with a view to achieving economic growth and positive social impact. This is the start of a long journey of a model that could be replicated for other cooperatives in Egypt.

The road ahead still entails changing the prevailing culture of small growers into one of collaborative demand/market-driven operations with a strong export orientation focused on clean and organic farming to produce safe food. The main challenge for Dakrouri, after proving the concept on small scale, is to reach a scale necessary to render the model economical and competitive with other large growers. Over the past years of implementation, considerable experience was gained in change management—in introducing a new agriculture and development culture. Results show progressive growth, with some market challenges. Performance is measured by the value-added services offered and by how many Egyptian pounds the program has been able to provide each farmer, for each ton of produce he or she has delivered through the system, over the market price and from an increase in productivity. Despite all the obstacles and challenges the program faced, it was able to grow from forty farmers in the 2006–2007 production year to two hundred farmers in 2010–11 (the number later went down to 126 as a result of market circumstances). Critical volume is slow to achieve, due to the inability to find enough seeds for all growers, among other market factors, mainly from a drop in prices. The success so far is significant, however, and has built confidence in the program, which is a strong basis for expansion. For the buyers the program has delivered products to their exact requirements from the first delivery. This reliability of service and product has paved the way for sustainability and trust.

References

Bender, A.D., et al. 1990. "Entrepreneurship Education and Micro Business Development as a Part of a Program of Community Revitalization." *Economics Development Review* 8, no. 1: 38–41.

Bornstein, D., and S. Davis. 2010. *Social Entrepreneurship: What Everyone Needs to Know.* New York: Oxford University Press.

Dakrouri, A. 2014. Presentation on APVC Model. Logistics Academy, International Excutive Education Institute, American University in Cairo, February 2014.

Davidsson, P. 1989. "Entrepreneurship and After? A Study of Growth Willingness in Small Firms." *Journal of Business Venturing* 4, no. 3: 210–26.

Drayton, B., and Valeria Budinich. 2010. "A New Alliance for Global Change." *Harvard Business Review*, September, 57–64.

Hammond, A. 2010. "BoP Venture Formation for Scale." In *Next Generation Business Strategies for the Base of the Pyramid: New Approaches for Building Mutual Value*, edited by Ted London and Stuart Hart, 193–215. Upper Saddle River, NJ: FT Press.

Institute of National Planning. Egypt, 2008.

UNDP (United Nations Development Programme). 2005. *Egypt Human Development Report 2005*. United Nations Development Programme and The Institute of National Planning, Cairo, Egypt, 2005.

10 Transferring World Athletic Championship–Winning Principles to Entrepreneurship: The Case of Abdelkader El Mouaziz

Abderrahman Hassi, Khaoula Zitouni, and Omar Bacadi

Introduction

Abdelkader El Mouaziz is a renowned, award-winning Moroccan athlete recognized for leading races at the most famous marathons around the globe.[1] El Mouaziz holds one of the best performances in the marathon category and is noted for being the only athlete who has run thirteen marathons in record times of less than two hours and ten minutes. His best time was 2:06:46 at the Chicago Marathon in 2002. He is the winner of the Madrid Marathon in 1994, the London Marathon in 1999 and 2001, the New York Marathon in 2001, and the Marrakesh Marathon in Morocco in 1996, 1997, and 1999.[2] Moreover, El Mouaziz was the top marathon athlete in 2001 and the runner-up winner in 2002 in the world.

While El Mouaziz was running for the Moroccan national team, he spent most of his time training in the mountain hills of the Ifrane-Azrou region, a resplendent area appreciated for its altitude, airy cedar forests, and pure, refreshing air surrounded by nature's stillness and tranquility.

The 45-year-old runner is an accomplished athlete who also displays a strong entrepreneurial spirit. After winning numerous international competitions and officially retiring from competitive running, he left his native Casablanca to return to the Ifrane-Azrou region, where he settled and started a small business, employing a handful of individuals from the Atlas region. El Mouaziz wanted to give back by paying tribute to the region that nurtured and helped him to become a sporting legend. With the intention of generating viable economic activity, he ventured into a small business that would create jobs and employ the local people. The 'Champion des Cèdres'[3] aimed to improve the living conditions of the modest people of this particular and exceptional Middle Atlas region.

El Mouaziz manages his business the same way he managed his athletic career. In fact, his management style is based on principles inspired and spurred by his professional athletic career. These values include performance, fair play, competitiveness, perseverance, hard work, and collaboration.

One of the unique traits of El Mouaziz is his rooted intrinsic qualities that implicitly define success and enthusiasm. It is most interesting to pay close attention to his triumphant story and examine how he cultivated the foundations of his management practices from his learned experiences in sportsmanship. First, it is important to present a general overview of tourism in Morocco and in the Ifrane region.

Tourism in Morocco

Travel and tourism constitute an important industry in the Moroccan economy. It contributed MAD152.5 billion (US$18.46 billion) in 2011, which is 19 percent of the total GDP (World Travel and Tourism Council 2012). Foreign visitors and international tourism accounted for 70.5 percent of this industry's total contribution while domestic travel yielded 29.5 percent. Travel and tourism directly supported 834,500 jobs, which represents 7.8 percent of total employment in Morocco in 2011. In terms of investment, travel and tourism constituted 10.2 percent of total investment with an amount reaching MAD25.2 billion (US$3.5 billion) in 2011 (World Travel and Tourism Council 2012).

Ifrane Region

Nestled in the Middle Atlas mountains at an altitude of 1,600 meters (5,000 feet), Ifrane is the abode of the largest cedar forest in Africa. With hundreds of diverse birds, numerous reptile species inhabiting the plateaus, and unique, endangered monkeys dwelling in the cedars of the region, Ifrane is the most biologically diverse area in Morocco. The ski slopes of the Michlifen and Hebri mountains are less than twenty minutes from downtown and are ideal for winter activities or athletic training, as wintry temperatures remain pleasantly cool. Ifrane is also about 60 kilometers away from the imperial cities of Meknes and Fez, less than two hours from the capital city of Rabat and the Atlantic coast, and only a half-day's journey from the Sahara desert.

Ifrane is a picturesque village with a population of about 15,000 inhabitants that can easily expand to approximately 100,000 visitors on weekends and holidays during both the winter and summer seasons. Snow aficionados can take part in winter sports and activities such as downhill and cross-country skiing, snowboarding, or riding horses along the hills. Ifrane is also very much appreciated by national and international athletes who regularly train for days or even weeks in the region due to its altitude and unpolluted air. Ifrane has a climatic zone perfect for creating future world champions. There are 62 different accommodation facilities in Ifrane, creating a thousand jobs. Ifrane also hosts six major summer camps, representing 40 percent of total summer camps in the country. In 2012, 100,000 tourists visited Ifrane with a total of 150,000 overnights (Alami 2013).

Tourtite

In March 2010, El Mouaziz opened modest bed and breakfast (B&B) establishment called Tourtite. In the local Berber language, *tourtite* means 'garden.' Tourtite offers panoramic, breathtaking views of the Atlas gardens, the green of the Ras El Ma meadows, and mountain hills between the villages of Ifrane and Azrou. With his athletic experience in mind, El Mouaziz believed that the serious athlete who came to train in the Ifrane region lacked a suitable place to rest and revitalize during training. He came to the conclusion that a distinctive B&B would meet their exclusive needs.

Tourtite is designed for people who wholeheartedly embrace nature, athletes who would like to train in high mountain areas, and people who would like to spend their holidays off the tourist track. Located in a quiet area in the heart of nature with a family-oriented atmosphere, the B&B is the starting point for people to explore the region. First and foremost, Tourtite serves to train and nurture athletes and sportspeople. It also welcomes local residents for quiet, healthy meals with friends and family. Tourtite has twenty-four rooms and two suites with both rustic-style and modern equipment along with traditional and Berber artifacts from the south of Morocco.[4] It offers all the amenities of a small hotel, such as a restaurant, laundry room, a small park for children, and a fitness room with cardio training equipment. The B&B also provides transportation, with a 12-seat van to transport guests and visitors to sites around the region.

Tourtite's menu consists of traditionally prepared local meals such as Atlas trout, as well as à la carte items. Personalized meals are prepared on request for athletes on a high-caliber nutritional regimen. Most of the produce and foods are local and organic. There is also a *hamam* available for B&B guests. *Hamam*s are Moroccan-style traditional hot baths that are beneficial for athletes after long hours of rigorous training.

Tourtite has become a popular place for nature lovers because it provides a comforting environment where the proprietor and his employees work collaboratively to satisfy their B&B guests. Many people from different parts of Europe spend several days on a yearly basis at Tourtite. Visitors seem to enjoy its combination of tranquility and expertise in athletic training.

Training Camps

In addition to the bed and breakfast services, El Mouaziz provides training camps to regular guests, recreation seekers, passionate hikers, and professional athletes. After developing an agreed-upon training program, he meticulously implements it with the commitment of the clients. El Mouaziz personally trains clients in the mountains and provides them with the necessary support and advice, to enhance their performance, regardless of their ability.[5]

It should be noted that several world champions have trained on the track and trails of Ifrane to prepare for their competitions. They include the Algerian athlete Nouria Merah-Benida,[6] the Moroccan athlete Zahra Ouaziz, and the Romanian athlete Gabriela Szabo (Minshull 1999), the Ugandan athlete Julius Achon, the Moroccan athlete Hicham El Guerrouj, the British athlete Jon Wid, and the Qatar national track and field team (Velediaz 1999).

Over the years, El Mouaziz had often remarked that the region had an immense natural potential to attract amateur sportspeople and particularly professional runners. Driven by a desire to make things happen, he decided to put his experience in sports to use and design custom-tailored training programs for prospective athletic clients. The goal was to deliver well-balanced athletic regimens to amateurs as a course of therapy in professional running and sprinting, including the ideals of sportsmanship.

Cedar International Marathon

To promote environment-friendly sports in the region, and particularly marathon running, his own area of specialization, El Mouaziz established the Cedar International Marathon in the Ifrane region. During four days at the end of June each year, professional athletes and marathon enthusiasts run across the Ifrane cedar forest. The race takes place at high altitude, between 1,600 and 2,100 meters above sea level. Hundreds of marathon runners from all over the world participate in the competition every year, with the numbers of runners increasing from year to year. In 2013, participants came from Algeria, Belgium, Holland, Libya, Portugal, Canada, the United Kingdom, and the United States. The marathon is organized by the

Sport and Nature Association, presided over by El Mouaziz. The marathon coincides with World Environment Day, which also aims at promoting ecological and green tourism in the region. The prizes are MAD10,000 (US$1,200) for the winner, MAD7,000 (US$850) for the first runner-up, and MAD5,000 (US$600) for the second runner-up. There is also a five-kilometer race for youth (under 16 years old) to encourage young people to exercise and practice sports. The weather, ambiance, springs, and lakes allow for the combination of sports and tourism in the Ifrane region.

El Mouaziz has developed a special relationship with the Ifrane region. He sincerely believes that this region contributed tremendously to his success as a world champion marathon runner. His B&B employs people from the region, in whom he wants to instill a number of values that he believes were the secret behind his outstanding career. What are the factors and personal values of El Mouaziz that contributed to his smooth transformation from a marathon champion to a successful small-business entrepreneur?

El Mouaziz's Early Years

Abdelkader El Mouaziz comes from a modest, hard-working family in which he is the eldest son. He claims that his sense of entrepreneurship emerged at a very young age when he started to make toys for himself in order to be able to play with his friends. He could not afford to buy the toys he wanted from the market and had no choice but to produce them himself with available materials. Thus the former professional athlete has always been an entrepreneur, long before he started his professional career in sports. Being the only entrepreneur in his family, El Mouaziz believes that he was not influenced by anyone in his immediate surroundings. He did not receive any prior business training before opening his B&B or any support from others to start his business. The Tourtite idea was exclusively his.

El Mouaziz still has a vivid memory of the competitive environment in which he grew up: this feeling is one of the foundations of his tenacious spirit in sport and business that leads him to initiate things, take risks, and never fear the unknown, which embodies his personality and his management style. He believes that it was the environment of his early days that developed the values and principles that have shaped his destiny: competitiveness, perseverance, hard work, and collaboration. El Mouaziz particularly appreciates his physical education teachers who contributed to his professional athletic career: "I am always thankful for my sport instructors who made sacrifices one afternoon or two per week to train me and share their insights in regard to sport competitions. They were always there for me; that was a very strong commitment but a generous and beautiful one as well."[7]

El Mouaziz's family and instructors taught him about superior performance and the meaning of dedication, commitment, and devotion to a sport. Another important lesson they taught him was that no matter how challenging things appeared, the ultimate goal was never impossible. This encouraged him never to give up in competitions, because with determination, winning was always possible. He believes that once we have the courage to go through a difficult situation, we know that next time, we will be able to face even more difficult ones.

> The moment I reach a specific running time for a given distance, the next time I run this very same distance, I have no choice but at least to reach the same result or break my own record. Competitions have taught me that effort and deprivation are key components for success. Delayed gratification is quintessential to triumph and victory.

Behavioral Model of Leadership

What makes El Mouaziz a successful athletepreneur? His leadership style is based on definable and learnable behaviors without which excellence and performance are not possible.

Leadership enables leaders to change the minds of their subordinates and to move organizations forward to reach desired outcomes. There are several theoretical frameworks that have been developed to explain the ability of superiors to influence the behavior of subordinates and to convince them to pursue a given course of action.

Behavioral theories of leadership place the emphasis on what leaders and superiors do in terms of actions rather than their personal traits. According to this perspective, leadership can be learned. In this regard, leaders showcase two kinds of behaviors that help individuals and teams to achieve their desired goals (Judge, Piccolo, and Iles 2004). The first is consideration: leaders are considerate and supportive of subordinates' pursuit of personal goals. They provide positive reinforcement and encouragement and they settle disputes among subordinates. Leaders adopt relationships with their followers that are characterized by mutual trust, two-way communication, respect for employees' ideas, and empathy for subordinates. The second is initiating structure, through which leaders establish task-based relationships with their employees focusing on setting work objectives to be accomplished.

El Mouaziz's Engine for Success
Determination
What makes the professional athlete and the entrepreneur persevere despite the hurdles (in every meaning of the word) that the individual faces along the way? Self-determination plays a major role for El Mouaziz. It is an engine that leads him to go beyond himself in search of excellence in performance. El Mouaziz made his own choices in life, responding to his personal needs, including the need for independence and individuality. He has always regarded his behavior as an expression of the self. This provides him with a feeling of satisfaction, as he acts because of his passion for the activity or by virtue of principles to which he adheres. In short, El Mouaziz's self-determination, whether as a champion athlete or as a business entrepreneur, is a direct response to his personal, innermost needs, including those of performance and excellence.

El Mouaziz has always aimed for the top, and he continues to do so in his small business venture: "When I run a competition, I do not do it to end up in the tenth position! I do it to win! I have to persevere and work harder than my competitors." He practices a similar philosophy when it comes to his business ventures. The ultimate goal is to make it work, investing the effort required to obtain optimal results.

Intrinsic motivation
The passion for training both amateur and professional athletes is the driving force that has led El Mouaziz to explore this unique and customized business pursuit aimed at sports training, running activities and events, marathon races, and sporting competitions. He decided to open a B&B offering sports programs that include training regimens and activities for both professional and non-professional athletes in order to remain close to his passion for sports and competition. It is sport that motivates him, rather than the prospect of generating economic activity for the primary purpose of making money: "For some entrepreneurs, making money is a means to becoming rich; that's not my motivation for starting a business! I love helping others to accomplish their desired outcomes. Money should not be the main goal of an entrepreneur; when we work hard, money will come automatically!"

It is clear that El Mouaziz has intrinsic motivation. This explains his self-determination, the energy he invests, his perseverance, and his satisfaction upon accomplishing results. Success and performance originate from intrinsic motivation, which is rooted in the passion of the entrepreneur. Future entrepreneurs need to ask themselves the following question: What are the real motivations that stimulate my desire to start a business? Understanding their own motivational factors allows entrepreneurs to make necessary choices while paving the way for favorable conditions to emerge naturally.

Passion

Passion has definitely been a determining influence in the success of El Mouaziz. This passion leads him to direct his effort and his commitment to reach excellence. When he was training for marathon competitions, he would train in conditions of snow, rainfall, and extreme heat. His passion is not obsessive, however; it is dedication based on positive emotions that overflow into his performance. "I remember during my first experiences, I was the best of the group. I had to train more than some of my friends, I had to suffer, to come home extremely tired, but it was a pleasure to constantly improve and grow!"

Perseverance

El Mouaziz learned to put forward whatever effort was required to win, even if it meant suffering. Just as in his sports career, he learned how to lead in business. One cannot become a successful entrepreneur overnight. It takes learning experiences, going through difficult times, and making tough decisions, in order to obtain success as the ultimate reward. Success is not a given; it must be earned through dedication, endurance, and hard work.

El Mouaziz contends that the efforts he put into training to win marathons are comparable to the efforts he puts forth to become a successful entrepreneur. Entrepreneurs need to develop good business reflexes, to seize the right opportunities at the most opportune time, and to invest the right amount of energy and resources. Entrepreneurs can make mistakes in the beginning of their venture, just like the amateur athlete. One needs to learn from these mistakes or, rather, valuable experiences, by using them to develop essential skills. Errors may just be indicative of the fact that the choices you made require further development or perhaps a slight redirection. Mistakes may indicate a need for change. Although they appear to be devastating and are perceived as failures, they may in fact be primary conditions required before the great win.

In El Mouaziz's case, it is evident that perseverance, hard work, deprivation, and self-motivation are key constituents for success. Passion is a key success factor for El Mouaziz, notably the taste of competition and the pleasurable sensation that it brings.

These factors need to be combined to produce an optimal level of performance rather than posing an obstacle that causes failure. The entrepreneur needs to make the right decision at the right moment. Emotions are an integral part of life of both the entrepreneur and the athlete: there are moments of joy and success as well as moments of anxiety and anguish. Entrepreneurs dread making poor decisions for fear of not making a success of it. Hence the importance of managing emotions well in the pursuit of objectives and goals.

Sport-related Techniques as Valuable Transferable Skills for Business

El Mouaziz has transferred an athletic technique into the business sphere: benchmarking. He sets entrepreneurial goals and objectives from beginning to end by observing and measuring competitors through various practices and sources such as local publications, word of mouth, and discussions with friends across the country and abroad.

El Mouaziz also uses the mental conditioning technique that he used as an athlete to improve his business performance. It consists of controlling emotions and behavior by means of a kind of military-style training regimen that includes going through training in the Atlas Mountains and, most importantly, struggling with deprivation. This practice yielded an exceptional athlete and a business champion. El Mouaziz learned how to efficiently manage stress, effectively handle the decision-making process, and adequately direct the strength of self-motivation. These qualities are mandatory prerequisites for successful entrepreneurs. They have made El Mouaziz's entrepreneurial journey easier than that of the average entrepreneurs as he learned to develop thick skin and become tenacious, to give the best of what he is, and to never give up what he sincerely believes in. It is that extra mile at the end of the line that makes or breaks the race, just like in business. Determination and perseverance take you over the winning line.

Just like the athlete, the entrepreneur must run hundreds or thousands of marathons before winning a competition! Personally, I learned to suffer through running. I had to fail many times before I began winning! My entire business model is based on my athletic life. My career as an athlete adequately prepared me for my entrepreneurial life.

Positive stress is a catalyst for success. Although stress is felt by anyone confronted with danger or a threat, it takes a special form for people who go through risky situations such as athletes and entrepreneurs. El Mouaziz admits experiencing what he calls "positive stress" during his career as an athlete as well as during his entrepreneurial career.

> I remember going through moments of stagnation as I stressed over the idea of not being able to win some competitions: I worked harder and harder but I was not able to significantly improve my performance. I feared being out of competitions and not winning! I navigated that challenging phase of my journey well. As an entrepreneur, I experience the same feeling from time to time: I fear making the wrong decision related to my business. But thanks to Allah, I make well-thought-out decisions and find myself on the right path every time.

El Mouaziz learned how to live life with a healthy dose of stress. He does not try to repress any of the strains that come to him but aims to control pressures, tensions, and anxieties to alleviate their impact on his physical and mental states. Both entrepreneurs and athletes ought not to negate or deny stress but should deal with it straightforwardly. By ignoring tensions, individuals can not see and adequately estimate threats around them and ultimately destabilize their equilibrium and fall. They should be humble enough not to believe that they are invincible and should keep in mind that everything and everyone is replaceable. There is a level of positive stress that helps attain certain levels of performance; we need to live with it, control it, manage it well, and most importantly, admit that it exists and accept it.

In both his athletic and entrepreneurial life, over the years El Mouaziz has developed a sense of risk-minimizing through calculated behaviors. He knows that the slightest mistake may cost him a title or a prize. He underwent serioius training with a family that functioned as a role model and a sport that shaped his mind. The former defined his principles, the latter defined the man he has become. One of the particularities of El Mouaziz is that he strongly believes in recuperating and relaxing after every effort. As an athlete, El Mouaziz always seeks physical and mental equilibrium after an exercise or a competition in order to recuperate adequately. To do this, he goes to a remote area in the mountains where he spends quiet time. As an entrepreneur, he pauses from time to time during the day for a cup of coffee or tea to relax and reflect on day-to-day decisions and operations. He finds refuge in his small cottage in the heart of the mountains, where he escapes for a weekend or even for a single day. This practice allows him to restore strength and find calmness, especially for a normally hyperactive individual like himself. This kind of relaxation is a crucial preventive measure to avoid the loss of positive emotions and performance. It is also vital to the overall well-being of the individual. The balance of mind, body, and soul is essential to great physical and mental form.

El Mouaziz has also adopted several other significant techniques from his professional sports career, such as setting objectives, developing a vision, and observing the environment. These strategies proved to be just as valid in the world of business as they were for a professional athlete.

Original Management Style

It goes without saying that, as a world champion, El Mouaziz did not need to start a small business in the middle of the Atlas Mountains. He wanted to give back and contribute to the betterment of other people's lives, in genuine commitment to true sport. He also wanted to bring together communities, groups, and organizations who want to ensure that sports offer a safe, welcoming, and rewarding experience for everyone. Raising awareness of the importance of protecting and embracing our environment and advancing green tourism are also very important to El Mouaziz. In short, his values of altruism and gratitude fundamentally motivated his start-up business and his involvement in both the association and the organization of the marathon competition. These qualities have led him to take advantage of business opportunities and set up not-for-profit activities. El Mouaziz despises greed and believes that gradual and progressive development is the key to success and sound sustainable growth.

The main challenge that El Mouaziz has always faced is developing a customer base. To meet this challenge, he takes part in all the activities of the business to get closer to his guests and employees, by building on a relationship based on trust with the former and collaboration with the latter. The runner sees himself and his employees as part of one working unit with a common purpose, which is to give Tourtite's customers the greatest possible experience. They proactively collaborate and participate in problem solving and decision-making processes using open, respectful, and constructive communication. Tourtite's work practices and environment encourage feedback and open communication for both employees and customers. To develop a customer base, El Mouaziz believes in carefully managing his own personal brand. He showcases what his B&B can offer potential guests, particularly athletes, whenever he gets a chance to do so.

Tourtite's management is driven by the values of the founder, El Mouaziz. His employees and business partners say that he cares most about excellence, honesty, fairness, collaboration, fair play, and well-being. In order to bring these values to life, El Mouaziz had to work hard in the beginning to rally his team around them. The adoption of these values also led his association to organize the International Cedar Marathon to ensure that participants, volunteers, and members receive the best possible sport experience. At Tourtite, everyone refers to these values to help make better decisions, to structure their tasks, to set priorities, and to efficiently manage difficult situations; hence the positive outcome, including achieving the majority of the strategic objectives of the business. As one of his employees puts it, "the El Mouaziz management approach has given his business a competitive edge by creating a sustainable, highly motivated, and energetic culture."

Tourtite has integrated values such as collaboration rather than top-down control techniques, competitiveness, fair play, and employee well-being in its culture and work procedures. Moreover, his simplicity, sincerity, and credibility have assisted El Mouaziz in promoting Tourtite locally, nationally, and internationally. These qualities have also helped him gain an advantage over the competition and assure guest satisfaction. And it is working well; results and performance are great. In the words of a former employee: "I've worked with El Mouaziz for a while; I have to say that his management style is not only about publicly preaching what his values are; it is a concrete and genuine approach that consists of transforming these values into practices and actions."

Competitiveness

As an individual, El Mouaziz is a dynamic, passionate, and dedicated individual, and outstandingly success-driven. He has created a corporate culture that is employee-centered, values-driven, and most importantly, excellence-oriented. As a seasoned athlete, he contends that any business path is riddled with challenges that make achieving success difficult but not impossible. He transferred these sportsmanship values to business and he continuously influences his employees to adhere to these values. El Mouaziz sees high risk as an integral part of any business. He jokingly gives the example of marathon competitions where "hundreds or thousands of athletes participate but only three of them win the competition! One of the ways to win is to set objectives . . . and to strive to reach them; only hard work and perseverance can help make it happen."

Collaboration

In managing individuals in a workplace setting, El Mouaziz believes that adhering to humanistic standards will help to retain the right people over the long term, keep the focus on achieving results, and attract new, highly qualified and motivated members to a business. His employees are qualified, competent, and caring individuals who walk the talk, believe in El Mouaziz's and Tourtite's values, and reflect them in their everyday practices and operations. They make consistent decisions and act with good faith, and consequently are rewarded and appreciated by the leader, as one of them states:

> At Tourtite, employees' values are congruent with the core values of El Mouaziz and the B&B, the result is contentment and satisfaction which, in turn, enhance performance and the general well-being of his employees. And for these simple reasons, everyone is loyal to him and will always be forever grateful.

Fair play

Fair play is a value that characterizes El Mouaziz's leadership approach. He commits vehemently to fairness in daily activities and always makes sure that the appropriate procedures and policies are enforced, be it in his hiring practices, remuneration schemes, or communication style. When conflicts arise between employees, they are resolved before they even begin, thanks to his proactive approach, as there is a fair, clear, and efficient system in place to deal with any kind of dispute in a satisfactory and objective manner.

Well-being

El Mouaziz always maintains a respectful environment for employees and clients. There are feedback forms and suggestion boxes to ensure a positive environment for the exchange of ideas. He rewards respectful behavior at all levels and ensures that new employees are selected based not only on their technical skills and competencies but also because they share the business philosophy.

Employees maintain a healthy balance between work and their personal life. Tourtite is about a state of wellness, as El Mouaziz pays close attention to the physical and emotional well-being of his employees. He encourages his employees to take time off and hence employees are fit and relaxed, with no one ever complaining that he or she is overworked.

Tourtite adopts healthy practices and invests in its human capital through a variety of practices such as performance-related incentives and by creating a culture that values employees' positive contribution. One of his former employees compared working for El Mouaziz with one of his previous jobs and noted that:

> At my former work, which is located in the Ifrane region as well, there was a complete absence of organizational values; employees relied on their personal convictions to complete their tasks and inform their decision-making. This lack in the organization's values became, with time, a breeding ground for increased conflict among employees, inconsistent results, and ultimately, a fragmented organizational culture. We don't see that at an El Mouaziz work environment. It is the extreme opposite!

Nonetheless, sometimes employees abuse El Mouaziz's trust and benevolence, which makes him question his use of a standardized approach to treating employees; he wonders whether resorting to a case-by-case approach would be more efficient.

Conclusion

Abdelkader El Mouaziz's business and sport activities in the Ifrane region were driven by a giving-back-to-the-community motivation, which is reflected in the thousand things he does that show how much he cares about the community he lives in. In the cause of sport, he was able to rally the entire community around green sport, as he tries to put in place a culture that fosters building up sport as a valued public asset. In business, he established a bed and breakfast with a homelike feel to it that employs numerous individuals from the region and that is managed on the basis of solid principles and values. To succeed in business, El Mouaziz emphasizes the importance of being honest, humble, and ambitious, with clearly defined ideas as essential focus points.

El Mouaziz transfers his sports values and principles into the business management of Tourtite. Honesty, competitiveness, collaboration, fairness, and hard work are very important values in his daily activities. In every situation, he works hard to enforce those values while encouraging his employees to adhere to them, wholeheartedly believing that these principles lead to success. For El Mouaziz, being ethical is the best way to build and sustain success. Further, by truly applying and respecting these values, his employees feel comfortable working for him. He treats them not as his employees but as his extended family, and this is a source of motivation for them. Sometimes some employees abuse this trust and benevolence, which makes him question his use of a standardized approach of treating employees; he wonders whether a case-by-case approach would be more efficient.

El Mouaziz is a very passionate and success-driven person. He believes that challenges, even high-risk ones, are part of the equation of real success. El Mouaziz also deeply believes that perseverance and hard work are key factors for success, and tries to influence his employees to embrace those values.

As in the sports world, fairness is also very important for Abdelkader El Mouaziz when managing his businesses. The marathon champion tries to be fair when implementing rules, taking decisions, hiring suitable staff, giving salaries, distributing rewards, or enforcing reprimands and warnings. He doesn't play favorites and treats everyone the same. To better understand the success of athletes, the concept of "fit" between the person and the endeavor is of crucial importance. The better the fit is, the more likely the chance for an individual to achieve full performance potential. El Mouaziz's story is a perfect example of this. Consistency between what a person is and what a person does explains their success. Every individual who aspires to achieve full potential should search for this consistency and fit. This is not possible without thorough insights about what individuals possess as acquired knowledge, their values, principles, personal passions, and the intrinsic and extrinsic motivations that stimulate and guide them to strive for success.

Notes

1   The authors are grateful to Professor Giovanna Storti for her valuable comments on the first draft of this case study.
2   http://www.iaaf.org/athletes/morocco/
    abdelkader-el-mouaziz-20272#progression
3   French expression meaning 'Champion of Cedars,' sometimes used to describe him.
4   http://www.aubergetourtite.com/index1.html
5   http://www.runninginspired.co.uk/Training_Camps_with_EL_MOUAZIZ.html
6   http://archive.today/PX1PX
7   All quotations from Abdelkader El Mouaziz are taken from interviews conducted with him by the authors between February and April 2014.

References

Alami, Y.S. 2013. "Ifrane: Grand rush sur la petite Suisse." *L'Economiste*, 9 January. http://www.marocpress.com/fr/leconomiste/article-29641.html

Benyo, R., and J. Henderson. 2001. *Running Encyclopedia: The Ultimate Source for Today's Runner*. Champaign, IL: Human Kinetics

Judge, T.A., R.F. Piccolo, and R. Iles. 2004. "The Forgotten Ones? The Validity of Consideration and Initiating Structure in Leadership Research." *Journal of Applied Psychology* 89, no. 1: 36–51.

"Marathon de Londres: El Mouaziz, l'infatigable." 2001. Afrik.com, 25 April. http://www.afrik.com/article2656.html

Minshull, P. 1999. "Szabo Prevails Again over Close Friend." Reuters, 27 August. http://www.oocities.org/~dagmawi/NewsAug99/News_Aug29_Track.html

Rowlerson, G. 2009. *Moroccan Success: The Kada Way*. London: Chipmunka Publishing.

Veledíaz, M. 1999. "Hicham El Guerrouj's Training for the 1997 Season." Run-Down.com. http://run-down.com/guests/mv_el_guerrouj.php

Wirz, J. 2005. *Paul Tergat: Running to the Limit: His Life and His Training Secrets, with Many Tips for Runners*. Aachen: Meyer & Meyer.

World Travel and Tourism Council. 2012. "Travel and Tourism. Economic Impact 2012 Morocco." London: World Travel and Tourism Council.